PRACTICING TO TAKE THE

GRE®

GENERAL

TEST – No. 5

VERBAL QUANTITATIVE ANALYTICAL VERBAL QUANTITATIVE ANALYTICAL VERBAL QUANTITATIVE ANALYTICAL

INCLUDES:

- Three General Tests administered in 1986-87
- Instructions and answer sheets
- Percent of examinees answering each question correctly

AN OFFICIAL PUBLICATION OF THE GRE BOARD

Published by Educational Testing Service
for the Graduate Record Examinations Board

The Graduate Record Examinations Program offers a General Test measuring verbal, quantitative, and analytical abilities and Subject Tests measuring achievement in the following seventeen fields:

Biology	French	Music
Chemistry	Geology	Physics
Computer Science	History	Political Science
Economics	Literature in	Psychology
Education	English	Sociology
Engineering	Mathematics	Spanish

The tests are administered by Educational Testing Service under policies determined by the Graduate Record Examinations Board, an independent board affiliated with the Association of Graduate Schools and the Council of Graduate Schools in the United States.

The Graduate Record Examinations Board has made available for purchase two official practice books, each containing three General Tests, of which this book is one. The Board has also made available one full-length edition of each of the following Subject Tests: Biology, Chemistry, Computer Science, Economics, Education, Engineering, Geology, History, Literature in English, Mathematics, Physics, Psychology, and Sociology. The Subject Test practice books and *Practicing to Take the General Test — No. 4* may be purchased by using the order form on page 165.

Full-length editions of the other Subject Tests are not yet available. However, individual booklets describing each test and including sample questions and score interpretation information are available free of charge for all seventeen Subject Tests. The *GRE Information Bulletin,* also available free of charge, contains the General Test that was administered in December 1981 and several examples of each type of question used in the test with explanations of how the answers are derived. Copies of the *Bulletin* and the Subject Test Descriptive Booklets may be requested by writing to:

Graduate Record Examinations Program
CN 6014
Princeton, NJ 08541-6014

In association with Warner Books, Inc., a Warner Communications Company

USA: 0-446-38594-8
CAN: 0-446-38595-6

CONTENTS

PRACTICING TO TAKE THE GRE GENERAL TEST

The General Test is intended to measure verbal, quantitative, and analytical skills developed throughout your life. Although a brief review will not dramatically change the abilities you have acquired over years, use of this book may help you evaluate your ability level and identify areas for further study before you take the General Test.

This practice book contains the three GRE® General Tests that were given at GRE test centers in December 1986, February 1987, and June 1987. The tests are complete except for the single section in each test that was not counted in the scoring. The location of the nonscored section varies from test to test. So, when you take the General Test to earn scores, the sections may not be in the same order as these tests are.

The practice book also contains detailed descriptions of the nine types of questions used in the General Test and suggested strategies for answering them. Forty-eight sample questions with explanations illustrate these strategies.

On the following pages are suggestions for the use of this practice book. To obtain maximum benefit, try the following:

- Take the first test, score it, and compare your scores with the scores of other people who took the test.

- Read the practice material on pages 5-20.

- Take the second test, score it, and compare these scores with your previous scores to note your improvement and any persistent areas of weakness.

- Review again the sample questions and explanations related to the problems you've encountered. This will help guide you to further study.

- When you are ready, take the third test. The scores you earn on this test are the best estimate of what your performance might be if you take the General Test under standard conditions in the near future.

TEST-TAKING STRATEGY

Your test taking strategy may affect your scores. In preparing to take the General Test, it is important that you become thoroughly familiar with the directions in the practice tests because they are the same as those in the test you will take to earn scores. Once you have done this, it is still necessary to read the directions for each group of questions carefully during the actual test administration.

Work as rapidly as you can without being careless. Check frequently to make sure you are marking your answers in the appropriate rows on your answer sheet. Since no question carries greater weight than any other, do not spend too much time pondering questions you find extremely difficult or unfamiliar.

Your scores on the General Test will be determined by the number of best answers you select from the choices given. No penalty is assessed for incorrect answers. Therefore, even if you are uncertain about a question, it is better that you guess at the answer than not respond at all.

PROCEDURES FOR PRACTICING

To get an idea of your performance at this time, before further review, take the first practice test under conditions that simulate those at an actual test administration and evaluate the results.

Allow yourself 30 minutes to complete each section of the test. Work on only one section of the test during each 30 minute time period. Do not go back to a previous section or work on a subsequent section. (If you do so at an actual test administration, you may be dismissed from the test.) Once you have completed the third section of the test, you may take a 10- to 15-minute break.

Do not use dictionaries or other books, compasses, rulers, slide rules, calculators, calculator/watch combinations, or any other aids since you will not be permitted to use them at a test center.

When you are ready to begin the test:

- Remove an answer sheet from the back of this book.

- Read the back cover of the test book (page 64) and complete the identification portion of the answer sheet.

- Read the inside back cover of the test book (page 63).

- Note the time and begin testing.

Once you have completed the test, determine your score and evaluate your performance, following the procedures outlined under the next two headings. If you find weakness in any types of questions, review the relevant sample questions and explanations. When you are ready, take the second test following the same procedures as you did with the first. Repeat the process of scoring and evaluation to determine if your practice proved beneficial. If you still note weakness, review again those sample questions and explanations and undertake whatever further study and review you consider necessary. When you are ready to take the third test, again try to simulate actual testing conditions. Take the test, score your answer sheet, and convert the scores. These scores are the best estimate of what your performance might be if you register for and take the General Test in the near future.

Data on the General Test show that scores often rise, usually only by a small amount, as a result of taking the test more than once, although scores of some examinees do decline. By preparing to take the General Test as we have suggested here, you may be able to do better than you would if you took the test without any initial preparation.

HOW TO SCORE YOUR PRACTICE TEST

On the page following each test is a list of the correct answers. Match your answer to each question against the answer given in the list, crossing out questions you answered incorrectly or omitted. For test GR87-4, add the number of your correct answers in Sections 1 and 2 to obtain your raw verbal score, in Sections 3 and 4 to obtain your raw quantitative score, and in Sections 6 and 7 to obtain your raw analytical ability score. For test GR87-5, add the number of your correct answers in Sections 1 and 2 to obtain your raw verbal score, in Sections 3 and 4 to obtain your raw quantitative score, and in Sections 5 and 7 to obtain your raw analytical ability score. For GR87-6, add the number of your correct answers in Sections 1 and 2 to obtain your raw verbal score, in Sections 3 and 4 to obtain your raw quantitative score, and in Sections 5 and 6 to obtain your raw analytical ability score. In the conversion table for each test, you will find the scaled scores that correspond to your raw scores on that test. Convert your raw scores to scaled scores.

EVALUATING YOUR PERFORMANCE

To evaluate your performance, you may compare your scaled scores with those of others who have taken the General Test at GRE test centers since October 1, 1983. The score conversion tables on pages 66, 114, and 158 indicate for each scaled score shown, the percentages of examinees who earned lower scores. For example, in the table on page 66, in the percent column next to the verbal ability scaled score 460 is the percent 45. This means that 45 percent of the examinees tested between October 1, 1983, and September 30, 1986, earned verbal ability scores below 460. For each score you earned on this practice test, note the percent of GRE examinees who earned lower scores. This is a reasonable indication of your rank among GRE General Test examinees if you follow the test-taking suggestions in this practice book.

The P+ that appears to the right of the correct answer shown for each question in the test you have taken is based on the percent of examinees who actually took that edition of the test and answered the question correctly. (This percent, however, has been adjusted for differences in ability level of examinees tested at different administrations.) This information enables you to see how other examinees performed on each question. It can also help identify content areas in which you need more practice and review.

It is important to realize that ability patterns differ for people who have different interests and experience. The second table on page 158 shows you the average scores for people in various categories of intended graduate major fields. You can see that those whose interests lie in the physical sciences, which are highly mathematical, generally have relatively high scores in quantitative ability, whereas those interested in the humanities generally have relatively high verbal scores. Find the major field category most closely related to your career goal to see how your performance compares with that of others who are striving for similar goals.

ADDITIONAL INFORMATION

If you have any questions about any of the information in this book, please write to:

Graduate Record Examinations Program
CN 6000
Princeton, NJ 08541-6000

TEST PREPARATION MATERIAL

Purpose of the GRE General Test

The GRE General Test measures certain developed verbal, quantitative, and analytical abilities that are important for academic achievement. In doing so, the test necessarily reflects the opportunities and efforts that have contributed to the development of those abilities.

The General Test is only one of several means of evaluating likely success in graduate school. It is not intended to measure inherent intellectual capacity or intelligence. Neither is it intended to measure creativity, motivation, perseverance, or social worth. The test does, however, make it possible to compare students with different backgrounds. A GRE score of 500, for example, has the same meaning whether earned by a student at a small, private liberal arts college or by a student at a large public university.

Because several different forms (or editions) of the test are in active use, all students do not receive exactly the same test edition. However, all editions measure the same skills and meet the same specifications for content and difficulty. The scores from different editions are made comparable to one another by a statistical procedure known as equating. This process makes it possible to assure that all reported scores of a given value denote the same level of developed ability regardless of which edition of the test is taken.

Since students have wide-ranging backgrounds, interests, and skills, the *verbal sections* of the General Test use questions from diverse areas of experience. The areas range from the activities of daily life to broad categories of academic interest such as the sciences, social studies, and the humanities. Knowledge of high school level arithmetic, plane geometry, and algebra provides adequate preparation for the *quantitative sections* of the test. Questions in the *analytical sections* measure analytical skills developed in virtually all fields of study. No formal training in logic or methods of analysis is needed to do well in these sections.

How the Test is Developed

The General Test is composed of questions formulated by specialists in various fields. Each question is reviewed by several independent critics and revised if necessary. New questions are pretested in actual tests under standard testing conditions.

Questions appearing in a test for the first time are analyzed for usefulness and weaknesses; they are not used in computing scores. Questions that perform satisfactorily become part of a pool from which a new edition of the General Test will be assembled at a future date. Those that do not perform well are discarded or are rewritten to correct the flaws and tried out again.

When a General Test has been assembled, it is reviewed by other subject matter and test specialists from inside and outside ETS. After any problems raised in these reviews have been resolved, the test goes to a test editor, who may make further suggestions for change.

All reviewers except the editors, copyreaders, and proofreaders must attempt to answer each question without the help of the answer key. Thus, each reviewer "takes the test," uninfluenced by knowledge of what the question writer or test assembler believed each answer should be. The answer key is certified as official only after the reviewers have agreed independently on the best answer for each question.

The extensive procedure described above has been developed to assure that every question in the General Test is appropriate and useful and that the combination of questions is satisfactory. Even so, the appraisal is not complete until after the new edition has been administered worldwide and subjected to a rigorous item analysis to see whether each question yields the expected results.

Such an appraisal sometimes reveals that a question is not satisfactory after all. It may prove to be ambiguous, require information beyond the scope of the test, or be otherwise unsuitable. Answers to such a question are not used in computing scores.

Description of the General Test

In this description, several examples of each type of question included in the verbal, quantitative, and analytical measures of the GRE General Test are discussed and explanations of the correct answers are provided.

Verbal Ability

The verbal ability measure is designed to test one's ability to reason with words in solving problems. Reasoning effectively in a verbal medium depends primarily upon the ability to discern, comprehend, and analyze relationships among words or groups of words and within larger units of discourse such as sentences and written passages. Such factors as knowledge of words and practice in reading will, of course, define the limits within which one can reason using these tools.

The verbal measure consists of four question types: analogies, antonyms, sentence completions, and reading comprehension sets. The examples of verbal questions in this section do not reflect precisely the difficulty range of the verbal measure. A greater number of difficult questions than would be encountered in the test have been included to provide practice in approaching more complex verbal questions.

ANALOGIES

Analogy questions test the ability to recognize relationships among words and the concepts they represent and to recognize when these relationships are parallel. The process of eliminating four incorrect answer choices requires one to formulate and then analyze the relationships linking six pairs of words (the given pair and the five answer choices) and to recognize which answer pair is most nearly analogous to the given pair. Some examples of relationships that might be found in analogy questions are kind, size, contiguity, or degree.

Some approaches that may be helpful in answering analogy questions:

■ Before looking at the answer choices, try to establish a precise relationship between the words in the given pair. It is usually helpful to express that relationship in a phrase or sentence; for example, the relationship between the word pair THRIFTY : MISERLY could be expressed as "to be *miserly* is to be *thrifty* to an excessive degree." Next, look for the answer choice with the pair of words whose relationship is closest to that of the given pair and can be expressed in a similar fashion.

■ Occasionally, more than one of the answer choices may seem at first to express a relationship similar to that of the given pair. Go back to the given pair and try to state the relationship more precisely or identify some aspect of the relationship between the given pair of words that is paralleled in only *one* answer choice pair.

■ Remember that a single word can have several different meanings. If you are unable to establish a relationship between the given pair or to find a parallel relationship among the answer choice pairs, check to be sure you have not overlooked a possible second meaning for one of the words.

■ *Never* decide on the best answer without reading *all* the answer choices. If you do not read all the answer choices, you may miss an answer choice that would have appeared superior to the choice you made or might have prompted you to reevaluate your understanding of the question.

■ Practice recognizing and formulating relationships between word pairs. You can do this with the following sample questions and with the analogy questions in the practice test in this booklet.

Directions: **In each of the following questions, a related pair of words or phrases is followed by five lettered pairs of words or phrases. Select the lettered pair that best expresses a relationship similar to that expressed in the original pair.**

1. COLOR : SPECTRUM :: (A) tone : scale
(B) sound : waves (C) verse : poem
(D) dimension : space (E) cell : organism

The relationship between *color* and *spectrum* is not merely that of part to whole, in which case (E) or even (C) might be defended as correct. A *spectrum* is made up of a progressive, graduated series of colors, as a *scale* is of a progressive, graduated sequence of tones. Thus, (A) is correct. Here, the best answer must be selected from a group of fairly close choices.

2. ABDICATION : THRONE :: **(A)** paradox : argument **(B)** competition : match **(C)** defeat : election **(D)** bequest : will **(E)** resignation : office

The relationship between *abdication* and *throne* is easy to perceive and only the correct answer, (E), expresses a similar relationship. (C) is incorrect because *defeat* is not voluntary, as are *abdication* and *resignation* and because *election,* the process of attaining a particular status, is not parallel to *throne* and *office.*

3. DESICCATE : MOISTURE :: **(A)** pulverize : dust **(B)** varnish : deterioration **(C)** shatter : shards **(D)** bend : contents **(E)** darken : light

To *desiccate* an object is to cause it to dry up by depriving it of *moisture.* Among the answer choices, only (E) has a similar relationship between its two words: to *darken* an object is to make it darker by depriving it of *light.* In the other four choices, the first words, *pulverize, varnish, shatter,* and *bend,* are parallel to *desiccate* in that they describe actions that alter the condition of an object, but the second word is not something of which an object is deprived as a result of the action the first word describes. In (A) and (C), the second words, *dust* and *shards,* are the results of pulverizing and shattering, respectively. *Deterioration* in (B) may be prevented through varnishing, and *contents* in (D) bears no relationship to bending that resembles the relationship between *desiccate* and *moisture.*

4. HEADLONG : FORETHOUGHT :: **(A)** barefaced : shame **(B)** mealymouthed : talent **(C)** heartbroken : emotion **(D)** levelheaded : resolve **(E)** singlehanded : ambition

The difficulty of this question probably derives primarily from the complexity of the relationship between *headlong* and *forethought* rather than from any inherent difficulty in the words. Analysis of the relationship between *headlong* and *forethought* reveals the following: an action or behavior that is *headlong* reveals lack of *forethought.* Only answer choice (A) displays the same relationship between its two terms.

◼◼◼◼◼ ANTONYMS ◼◼◼◼◼

Although antonym questions test knowledge of vocabulary more directly than do any of the other verbal question types, the purpose of the antonym questions is to measure not merely the strength of one's vocabulary but also the ability to reason from a given concept to its opposite. Antonyms may require only rather general knowledge of a word or they may require one to make fine distinctions among answer choices. Antonyms are generally confined to nouns, verbs, and adjectives; answer choices may be single words or phrases.

Some approaches that may be helpful in answering antonym questions:

◼ Remember that you are looking for the word that is the most nearly *opposite* to the given word; you are *not* looking for a synonym. Since many words do not have a precise opposite, you must look for the answer choice that expresses a concept *most nearly* opposite to that of the given word. For this reason, antonym questions are not measures of rote vocabulary knowledge; rather, these questions ask you to evaluate shades of meaning and the interaction of meaning between words.

◼ In some cases more than one of the answer choices may appear at first to be opposite to the given word. Questions that require you to make fine distinctions among two or more answer choices are best handled by defining more precisely or in greater detail the meaning of the given word.

◼ It is often useful, in weighing answer choices, to make up a sentence using the given word; if you do not know the precise dictionary meaning of a word but have a general sense of how the word might be used, try to make up a phrase or sentence with the word. Substituting the answer choices in the phrase or sentence and seeing which best "fits," in that it reverses the meaning or tone of the sentence or phrase, may help you determine the best answer.

◼ Remember that a particular word may have more than one meaning, so if you are unable to find an answer choice that appears opposite to the given word, examine all the words for possible second meanings.

◼ Use your knowledge of root, prefix, and suffix meanings to help you determine the meanings of words with which you are not entirely familiar.

Directions: **Each question below consists of a word printed in capital letters followed by five lettered words or phrases. Choose the lettered word or phrase that is most nearly *opposite* in meaning to the word in capital letters. Since some of the questions require you to distinguish fine shades of meaning, be sure to consider all the choices before deciding which one is best.**

5. DIFFUSE : **(A)** concentrate **(B)** contend **(C)** imply **(D)** pretend **(E)** rebel

The answer is (A). *Diffuse* means to permit or cause to spread out; only (A) presents an idea that is in any way opposite to *diffuse.*

6. COINCIDENCE : **(A)** depletion **(B)** incongruity **(C)** pessimism **(D)** ill fortune **(E)** lack of ideas

One meaning of *coincidence* is being in harmony or accord; another is corresponding in nature, character, or function. *Incongruity,* the correct answer, means lack of harmony or lack of conformity. Answer choice (D) may seem plausible at first glance since a *coincidence* of events is often a pleasant chance occurrence ("good luck" as opposed to "bad luck"), but careful reflection reveals that a *coincidence* is not necessarily a positive phenomenon.

7. MULTIFARIOUS : **(A)** deprived of freedom **(B)** deprived of comfort **(C)** lacking space **(D)** lacking stability **(E)** lacking diversity

Multifarious means having or occurring in great variety, so the correct answer is (E). Even if one is not entirely familiar with the meaning of *multifarious,* it is possible to use the clue provided by "multi-" to help find the right answer to this question.

8. PARSIMONIOUS : **(A)** initial **(B)** vegetative **(C)** prodigal **(D)** affluent **(E)** impromptu

The answer to this question is (C); *parsimonious* means frugal to the point of stinginess, and *prodigal,* which means

7

extravagant to the point of wastefulness, is the only answer choice opposite in meaning. At first, answer choice (D), *affluent*, may seem plausible in that it may be thought that wealth is an opposite concept to frugality—but it is well known that not all wealthy persons are generous.

SENTENCE COMPLETIONS

The purpose of the sentence completion questions is to measure the ability to recognize words or phrases that both logically and stylistically complete the meaning of a sentence. In deciding which of five words or sets of words can best be substituted for blank spaces in a sentence, one must analyze the relationships among the component parts of the incomplete sentence. One must consider each answer choice and decide which completes the sentence in such a way that the sentence has a logically satisfying meaning and can be read as a stylistically integrated whole.

Sentence completion questions provide a context within which to analyze the function of words as they relate to and combine with one another to form a meaningful unit of discourse.

Some approaches that may be helpful in answering sentence completion questions:

■ Read the entire sentence carefully before you consider the answer choices; be sure you understand the ideas expressed in the sentence and examine the sentence for possible indications of tone (irony, humor, and the like).

■ Before reading the answer choices you may find it helpful to fill in the blanks with a word or words of your own that complete the meaning of the sentence. Then examine the answer choices to see if any of them parallels your own completion of the sentence.

■ Pay attention to grammatical clues in the sentence. For example, words like *although* and *nevertheless* indicate that some qualification or opposition is taking place in the sentence, whereas *moreover* implies an intensification or support of some idea in the sentence. Pay attention also to the style of, and choice of words in, the sentence; sometimes determining the best answer depends in whole or in part on considerations of stylistic consistency among the parts of the sentence.

■ If a sentence has two blanks, be sure that *both* parts of your answer choice fit logically and stylistically into the sentence. Do not choose an answer on the basis of the fit of the first word alone.

■ When you have chosen an answer, read the complete sentence through to check that it has acquired a logically and stylistically satisfying meaning.

Directions: Each sentence below has one or two blanks, each blank indicating that something has been omitted. Beneath the sentence are five lettered words or sets of words. Choose the word or set of words for each blank that *best* fits the meaning of the sentence as a whole.

9. Early ------- of hearing loss is ------- by the fact that the other senses are able to compensate for moderate amounts of loss, so that people frequently do not know that their hearing is imperfect.

(A) discovery . . indicated
(B) development . . prevented
(C) detection . . complicated
(D) treatment . . facilitated
(E) incidence . . corrected

The statement that the other senses compensate for partial loss of hearing indicates that the hearing loss is not *prevented* or *corrected*; therefore, choices (B) and (E) can be eliminated. Furthermore, the ability to compensate for hearing loss certainly does not facilitate the early *treatment* (D) or the early *discovery* (A) of hearing loss. It is reasonable, however, that early *detection* of hearing loss is *complicated* by the ability to compensate for it. The correct answer is (C).

10. The ------- science of seismology has grown just enough so that the first overly bold theories have been -------.

(A) magnetic . . accepted
(B) fledgling . . refuted
(C) revolutionary . . analyzed
(D) predictive . . protected
(E) exploratory . . recalled

At first reading, there may appear to be several answer choices that "make sense" when substituted in the blanks of the sentence. (A) and (D) can be dismissed fairly readily when it is seen that *accepted* and *protected* are not compatible with *overly bold* in the sentence. The sentence yielded by (C) is logically more acceptable but not as strong as the sentences yielded by (B) and (E). Of these two latter choices, (B) is superior on stylistic grounds: theories are not *recalled* (E), and *fledgling* (B) reflects the idea of growth present in the sentence.

11. If her characters are still being written about as unfathomable riddles, it is to be attributed more to a human passion for ------- than to dubious complexities of her art.

(A) conundrums   (B) platitudes   (C) scapegoats
(D) euphemisms   (E) stereotypes

The answer to this question is (A). While any of the answer choices may be argued to be an object of human passion, only *conundrums* enables the sentence *as a whole* to acquire a coherent meaning. It is necessary, in choosing an answer, to complete the sentence in such a way as to make clear why the writer's characters are seen as *unfathomable riddles*. A human penchant for *conundrums,* or puzzling questions whose answers can only be conjectural, will account for this.

READING COMPREHENSION

The purpose of the reading comprehension questions is to measure the ability to read with understanding, insight, and discrimination. This type of question explores the examinee's ability to analyze a written passage from several perspectives, including the ability to recognize both explicitly stated elements in the passage and assumptions underlying statements or arguments in the passage as well as the implications of those statements or arguments. Because the written passage upon which reading comprehension questions are based presents a sustained discussion of a particular topic, there is ample context for analyzing a variety of relationships; for example, the function of a word in relation to a larger segment of the passage, the relationships among the various ideas in the passage, or the relation of the author to his or her topic or to the audience.

There are six types of reading comprehension questions. These types focus on (1) the main idea or primary purpose of the passage; (2) information explicitly stated in the passage; (3) information or ideas implied or suggested by the author; (4) possible application of the author's ideas to other situations; (5) the author's logic, reasoning, or persuasive techniques; and (6) the tone of the passage or the author's attitude as it is revealed in the language used.

In each edition of the General Test, there are two relatively long reading comprehension passages, each providing the basis for answering seven or eight questions, and two relatively short passages, each providing the basis for answering three or four questions. The four passages are drawn from four different subject matter areas: the humanities, the social sciences, the biological sciences, and the physical sciences.

Some approaches that may be helpful in answering reading comprehension questions:

■ Since reading passages are drawn from many different disciplines and sources, you should not expect to be familiar with the material in all the passages. However, you should not be discouraged by encountering material with which you are not familiar; questions are to be answered on the basis of the information provided in the passage, and you are not expected to rely on outside knowledge, which you may or may not have, of a particular topic. You may, however, want to do last a passage that seems to you particularly difficult or unfamiliar.

■ There are different strategies for approaching reading comprehension questions; you must decide which works most effectively for you. You might try different strategies as you do the reading comprehension questions in the practice test in this booklet. Some different strategies are: reading the passage very closely and then proceeding to the questions; skimming the passage, reading quickly through the questions, and then rereading the passage closely; and reading the questions first, then reading the passage closely. You may find that different strategies work better for different kinds of passages; for example, it might be helpful with a difficult or unfamiliar passage to read through the questions first.

■ Whatever strategy you choose, you should analyze the passage carefully before answering the questions. As with any kind of close and thoughtful reading, you should be sensitive to clues that will help you understand less explicit aspects of the passage. Try to separate main ideas from supporting ideas or evidence; try also to separate the author's own ideas or attitudes from information he or she is simply presenting. It is important to note transitions from one idea to the next and to examine the relationships among the different ideas or parts of the passage: Are they contrasting? Are they complementary?, for example. You should consider both the points the author makes and the conclusions he or she draws and also how and why those points are made or conclusions drawn.

■ You may find it helpful to underline or mark key parts of the passage. For example, you might underline main ideas or important arguments or you might circle transitional words that will help you map the logical structure of the passage (*although, nevertheless, correspondingly,* and the like) or descriptive words that will help you identify the author's attitude toward a particular idea or person.

■ Read each question carefully and be certain that you understand exactly what is being asked.

■ *Always* read all the answer choices before selecting the best answer.

■ The best answer is the one that most accurately and most completely answers the question being posed. Be careful not to pick an answer choice simply because it is a true statement; be careful also not to be misled by answer choices that are only partially true or only partially satisfy the problem posed in the question.

■ Answer the questions on the basis of the information provided in the passage and do not rely on outside knowledge. Your own views or opinions may sometimes conflict with the views expressed or the information provided in the passage; be sure that you work within the context provided by the passage. You should not expect to agree with everything you encounter in reading passages.

Directions: **The passage is followed by questions based on its content. After reading the passage, choose the best answer to each question. Answer all questions following the passage on the basis of what is *stated* or *implied* in the passage.**

Picture-taking is a technique both for annexing the objective world and for expressing the singular self. Photographs depict objective realities that already exist, though only the camera can disclose them. And
(5) they depict an individual photographer's temperament, discovering itself through the camera's cropping of reality. That is, photography has two antithetical ideals: in the first, photography is about the world and the photographer is a mere observer who counts for
(10) little; but in the second, photography is the instrument of intrepid, questing subjectivity and the photographer is all.

These conflicting ideals arise from a fundamental uneasiness on the part of both photographers and
(15) viewers of photographs toward the aggressive component in "taking" a picture. Accordingly, the ideal of a photographer as observer is attractive because it implicitly denies that picture-taking is an aggressive act. The issue, of course, is not so clear-cut. What
(20) photographers do cannot be characterized as simply predatory or as simply, and essentially, benevolent. As a consequence, one ideal of picture-taking or the other is always being rediscovered and championed.

An important result of the coexistence of these two
(25) ideals is a recurrent ambivalence toward photography's means. Whatever the claims that photography might make to be a form of personal expression on a par with painting, its originality is inextricably linked to the powers of a machine. The steady growth of these
(30) powers has made possible the extraordinary informativeness and imaginative formal beauty of many photographs, like Harold Edgerton's high-speed photographs of a bullet hitting its target or of the swirls and eddies of a tennis stroke. But as cameras
(35) become more sophisticated, more automated, some photographers are tempted to disarm themselves or to suggest that they are not really armed, preferring to

submit themselves to the limits imposed by premodern camera technology because a cruder, less high-
(40) powered machine is thought to give more interesting or emotive results, to leave more room for creative accident. For example, it has been virtually a point of honor for many photographers, including Walker Evans and Cartier-Bresson, to refuse to use modern
(45) equipment. These photographers have come to doubt the value of the camera as an instrument of "fast seeing." Cartier-Bresson, in fact, claims that the modern camera may see too fast.

This ambivalence toward photographic means
(50) determines trends in taste. The cult of the future (of faster and faster seeing) alternates over time with the wish to return to a purer past—when images had a handmade quality. This nostalgia for some pristine state of the photographic enterprise is currently
(55) widespread and underlies the present-day enthusiasm for daguerreotypes and the work of forgotten nineteenth-century provincial photographers. Photographers and viewers of photographs, it seems, need periodically to resist their own knowingness.

12. According to the passage, the two antithetical ideals of photography differ primarily in the

    (A) value that each places on the beauty of the finished product
    (B) emphasis that each places on the emotional impact of the finished product
    (C) degree of technical knowledge that each requires of the photographer
    (D) extent of the power that each requires of the photographer's equipment
    (E) way in which each defines the role of the photographer

The answer to this question is (E). Photography's two ideals are presented in lines 7-12. The main emphasis in the description of these two ideals is on the relationship of the photographer to the enterprise of photography, with the photographer described in the one as a passive observer and in the other as an active questioner. (E) identifies this key feature in the description of the two ideals—the way in which each ideal conceives or defines the role of the photographer in photography. (A) through (D) present aspects of photography that are mentioned in the passage, but none of these choices represents a primary difference between the two ideals of photography.

13. According to the passage, interest among photographers in each of photography's two ideals can be described as

    (A) rapidly changing
    (B) cyclically recurring
    (C) steadily growing
    (D) unimportant to the viewers of photographs
    (E) unrelated to changes in technology

This question requires one to look for comments in the passage about the nature of photographers' interest in the two ideals of photography. While the whole passage is, in a sense, about the response of photographers to these ideals, there are elements in the passage that comment specifically on this issue. Lines 21-23 tell us that the two ideals alternate in terms of their perceived relevance and value, that each ideal has

periods of popularity and of neglect. These lines support (B). Lines 24-26 tell us that the two ideals affect attitudes toward "photography's means," that is, the technology of the camera; (E), therefore, cannot be the correct answer. In lines 49-53, attitudes toward photographic means (which result from the two ideals) are said to alternate over time; these lines provide further support for B. (A) can be eliminated because, although the passage tells us that the interest of photographers in each of the ideals fluctuates over time, it nowhere indicates that this fluctuation or change is rapid. Nor does the passage say anywhere that interest in these ideals is growing; the passage does state that the powers of the camera are steadily growing (lines 29-30), but this does not mean that interest in the two ideals is growing. Thus (C) can be eliminated. (D) can be eliminated because the passage nowhere states that reactions to the ideals are either important or unimportant to viewers' concerns. Thus (B) is the correct answer.

14. Which of the following statements would be most likely to begin the paragraph immediately following the passage?

    (A) Photographers, as a result of their heightened awareness of time, are constantly trying to capture events and actions that are fleeting.
    (B) Thus the cult of the future, the worship of machines and speed, is firmly established in spite of efforts to the contrary by some photographers.
    (C) The rejection of technical knowledge, however, can never be complete and photography cannot for any length of time pretend that it has no weapons.
    (D) The point of honor involved in rejecting complex equipment is, however, of no significance to the viewer of a photograph.
    (E) Consequently the impulse to return to the past through images that suggest a handwrought quality is nothing more than a passing fad.

Answering this question requires one to think about where the discussion in the passage as a whole is moving and in particular where the final paragraph points. The last two paragraphs discuss the effect of the two ideals of photography on photographers' attitudes toward the camera. The final paragraph describes two such attitudes, or trends in taste (one in which the technology of today's camera is valued and one in which it is seen as a handicap), and tells us that these two attitudes alternate, with the second currently predominating. (B) and (E) can be eliminated because they both suggest that the first attitude will prevail, thus contradicting information in the last paragraph. (A) is not connected in any way to the discussion of attitudes toward the use of the present-day camera and so is not a good choice. (D) appears related to the previous material in the passage in that it discusses the second attitude; however, it introduces an idea—consideration of the viewer—that has not been developed in the passage. (C), the correct answer, is superior not only because it comments on the second attitude but also because it reiterates the idea that neither attitude will prevail. (C) is strengthened through its stylistic relation to earlier elements in the passage: the use of the word *weapons* recalls the references in lines 36 and 37 to photographers as *armed* with cameras.

Quantitative Ability

The quantitative sections of the General Test are designed to measure basic mathematical skills, understanding of elementary mathematical concepts, and ability to reason quantitatively and to solve problems in a quantitative setting. The mathematics required does not extend beyond that assumed to be common to the mathematics background of all examinees. There is a balance among the questions requiring arithmetic, algebra, and geometry.

ARITHMETIC

Questions classified as arithmetic can be answered by performing arithmetic operations on numbers (adding, subtracting, multiplying, dividing, and finding powers, roots of powers, percents, and averages), by reasoning, or by a combination of the two.

Some facts about numbers that might be helpful. An odd integer power of a negative number is negative, and an even integer power is positive; for example, $(-2)^3 = -8$, but $(-2)^2 = 4$.

Squaring a number between 0 and 1 (or raising it to a higher power) results in a smaller number; for example,

$(\frac{1}{2})^2 = \frac{1}{4}$ and $\frac{1}{4}$ is less than $\frac{1}{2}$.

The integers 0 and 1 have some properties that other numbers do not have; for example, the product of 0 and any number is 0, and the product of 1 and any number is that number.

ALGEBRA

The algebra required does not extend beyond that usually covered in a first-year high school course and includes such topics as properties of odd and even integers, divisibility, factors, and multiples in the system of integers, prime numbers, properties of signed numbers, linear equations and inequalities, factorable quadratic equations, factorization, simplification of algebraic expressions, exponents, and radicals. The skills required include the ability to solve simple equations, the ability to read and set up an equation for solving a complex problem, and the ability to apply basic algebraic skills to solve unfamiliar problems. It is expected that examinees will be familiar with symbols that are conventionally used in elementary algebra, such as the following: $x < y$ (this means that x is less than y), $x \neq y$ (this means that x is not equal to y), $|x|$ (this is defined to be x if $x > 0$ and $-x$ if $x < 0$), and $\sqrt{x^2}$ (this denotes the non-negative square root of x^2, that is, $\sqrt{x^2} = |x|$). Nonstandard notation is used only when it is explicitly defined for a particular question.

Some facts about algebra that might be helpful. The sum and product of even and odd integers will be even or odd depending on the operation and the kinds of integers; for example, the sum of an odd integer and an even integer is odd.

If an integer P is a divisor or a factor of another integer N, then N is the product of P and another integer and N is said to be an integer multiple of P; for example, 3 is a divisor or a factor of 6, and 6 is an integer multiple of 3.

A prime number is a number that has only two distinct positive divisors, 1 and itself; for example, 2, 3, and 5 are prime numbers, but $9 = 3 \cdot 3$ is not.

The sum and product of signed numbers will be positive or negative depending on the operation and the kinds of numbers; for example, the product of a negative number and a positive number is negative.

For any two numbers on the number line, the number on the left is less than the number on the right; for example, $2 < 3$ and $-4 < -3$.

Multiplying an inequality by a negative number reverses the direction of the inequality sign; for example, if the inequality $2 < 4$ is multipled by -2, the resulting inequality will be $-4 > -8$.

The two numbers $\sqrt{x^2}$ and $|x|$ are never negative; for example $\sqrt{3^2} = \sqrt{(-3)^2} = 3$ and $|-2| = -(-2) = 2$.

If $ab = 0$, then $a = 0$ or $b = 0$; for example, if $x^2 - 1 = 0$, then, since $x^2 - 1 = (x-1)(x+1)$, $(x-1)(x+1) = 0$ and therefore $x = 1$ or $x = -1$.

A positive integer exponent on a number indicates the number of times that number appears in the product; for example, x^4 means $x \cdot x \cdot x \cdot x$ and, therefore,

$$x^4 \cdot x^3 = (x \cdot x \cdot x \cdot x)(x \cdot x \cdot x) = x^7 \text{ or } \frac{x^4}{x^3} = \frac{x \cdot x \cdot x \cdot x}{x \cdot x \cdot x} = x.$$

GEOMETRY

The geometry questions are limited primarily to measurement and intuitive geometry or spatial visualization. Although a question may be posed in either English units or metric units of measure, the knowledge required for converting units in one system to units in another system or from one unit to another in the same system will not be tested. If an answer to a question is expected to be a unit of measure different from the unit in which the question is posed, a relationship between the units will be provided in the question. Topics include properties of lines, circles, triangles, rectangles, and other polygons; measurement-related concepts of area, perimeter, volume, and angle measure in degrees; and the Pythagorean theorem. Knowledge of simple coordinate geometry and special triangles such as isosceles, equilateral, and $30° - 60° - 90°$ triangles is also assumed. It is expected that examinees will be familiar with symbols that are conventionally used in elementary geometry, such as the following: $||$ (this means *is parallel to*), $\perp$ (this means *is*

perpendicular to), and (this means that $\angle ABC$ is a

right angle). The ability to construct proofs and knowledge of theorems that are usually learned only in a formal geometry course are not measured.

Some facts about geometry that might be helpful. If two lines intersect, the vertical angles are equal; for example, in the

figure , $x = y$.

If two parallel lines are intersected by a third line, some of the angles formed are equal; for example, in the figure

where $\ell_1 || \ell_2$, $y = x = z$.

The number of degrees of arc in a circle is 360; for example,

in the figure if $x = 60$, then the length of arc

ABC is $\frac{60}{360}$ of the circumference of the circle.

The sum of the degree measures of the angles of a triangle is 180.

The volume of a rectangular solid or of a right circular cylinder is the product of the area of the base and the height; for example, the volume of a cylinder with base of radius 2 and height 5 is $\pi\,(2^2)\,(5) = 20\pi$.

The square of the length of the hypotenuse of a right triangle is equal to the sum of the squares of the lengths of the two legs.

The coordinates of a point (x,y) give the location of the point in the coordinate plane; for example, the point $(2, -3)$ is located in the fourth quadrant 2 units to the right of the Y-axis and 3 units below the X-axis.

The sides of a $45° - 45° - 90°$ triangle are in the ratio $1 : 1 : \sqrt{2}$, and the sides of a $30° - 60° - 90°$ triangle are in the ratio $1 : \sqrt{3} : 2$.

Drawing in lines that are not shown in a figure can sometimes help in solving a geometry problem; for example, by drawing the dashed lines in the pentagon

, the number of degrees in the pentagon

can be found by adding up the number of degrees in the three triangles.

The quantitative measure employs three types of questions: quantitative comparison, discrete quantitative, and data interpretation. Pacing yourself on all of these question types is important. Do not spend an excessive amount of time pondering over problems you find difficult. Go on to the next question and, if time permits, come back to the difficult questions when you have completed the section.

The following information on numbers and figures applies to all questions in the quantitative sections.

Numbers: All numbers used are real numbers.

Figures: Position of points, angles, regions, etc. can be assumed to be in the order shown, and angle measures can be assumed to be positive.

Lines shown as straight can be assumed to be straight.

Figures can be assumed to lie in a plane unless otherwise indicated.

Figures that accompany questions are intended to provide information useful in answering the questions. However, unless a note states that a figure is drawn to scale, you should solve these problems NOT by estimating sizes by sight or by measurement, but by using your knowledge of mathematics.

▰▰▰▰▰QUANTITATIVE COMPARISON▰▰▰▰▰

The quantitative comparison questions test the ability to reason quickly and accurately about the relative sizes of two quantities or to perceive that not enough information is provided to make such a decision. To solve a quantitative comparison problem, you compare the quantities given in two columns, Column A and Column B, and decide whether one quantity is greater than the other, whether the two quantities are equal, or whether the relationship cannot be determined from the information given. Some questions only require

some manipulation to determine which of the quantities is greater; other questions require you to reason more or to think of special cases in which the relative sizes of the quantities reverse.

The following strategies might help in answering quantitative comparison questions.

- Do not waste time performing needless computations in order to eventually compare two specific numbers. Simplify or transform one or both of the given quantities only as much as is necessary to determine which quantity is greater or whether the two quantities are equal. Once you have determined that one quantity is greater than the other, do not take time to find the exact sizes of the quantities. Answer and go on to the next question.

- If both quantities being compared involve no variables, then the correct answer can never be (D), which states that the relationship cannot be determined. The answer is then reduced to three choices.

- Consider all kinds of numbers before you make a decision. As soon as you establish that quantity A is greater in one case while quantity B is greater in another case, choose answer (D) immediately and move on to the next comparison.

- Geometric figures may not be drawn to scale. Comparisons should be made based on knowledge of mathematics rather than appearance. However, you can sometimes find a clue by sketching another figure in your test book. Try to visualize the parts of a figure that are fixed by the information given and the parts that are collapsible and changeable. If a figure can flow into other shapes and sizes while conforming to given information, the answer is probably (D).

Directions for quantitative comparison questions and some examples with explanations follow.

Directions: Each of the following questions consists of two quantities, one in Column A and one in Column B. You are to compare the two quantities and choose

A if the quantity in Column A is greater;
B if the quantity in Column B is greater;
C if the two quantities are equal;
D if the relationship cannot be determined from the information given.

Note: Since there are only four choices, NEVER MARK (E).

Common Information: In a question, information concerning one or both of the quantities to be compared is centered above the two columns. A symbol that appears in both columns represents the same thing in Column A as it does in Column B.

	Column A	Column B	Sample Answers
Example 1:	2 × 6	2 + 6	● Ⓑ Ⓒ Ⓓ Ⓔ

Examples 2-4 refer to △PQR.

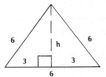

Example 2:	PN	NQ	Ⓐ Ⓑ Ⓒ ● Ⓔ

(since equal measures cannot be assumed, even though PN and NQ appear equal)

Example 3:	x	y	Ⓐ ● Ⓒ Ⓓ Ⓔ

(since N is between P and Q)

Example 4:	w + z	180	Ⓐ Ⓑ ● Ⓓ Ⓔ

(since PQ is a straight line)

Column A	Column B
15. 9.8	$\sqrt{100}$

$\sqrt{100}$ denotes 10, the positive square root of 100. (For any positive number x, $\sqrt{x}$ denotes the *positive* number whose square is x.) Since 10 is greater than 9.8, the correct answer is B. It is important not to confuse this question with a comparison of 9.8 and x where $x^2 = 100$. The latter comparison would yield D as the correct answer because $x^2 = 100$ implies that either $x = \sqrt{100}$ or $x = -\sqrt{100}$, and there is no way to determine which value x actually would have. However, this question asks for a comparison of 9.8 and $\sqrt{100}$, and $9.8 < \sqrt{100}$ for the reasons previously given.

Column A	Column B
16. $(-6)^4$	$(-6)^5$

Since $(-6)^4$ is the product of four negative factors and the product of an even number of negative numbers is positive, $(-6)^4$ is positive. Since the product of an odd number of negative numbers is negative, $(-6)^5$ is negative. Therefore $(-6)^4$ is greater than $(-6)^5$ since any positive number is greater than any negative number. The correct answer is A. Do not waste time determining that $(-6)^4 = 1,296$ and that $(-6)^5 = -7,776$. This information is not needed to make the comparison.

$$x + y = 10$$
$$x - y = 2$$

Column A	Column B
17. $x^2 - y^2$	19

Since $x^2 - y^2 = (x + y)(x - y)$ and, from the information given, $(x + y)(x - y) = 10 \cdot 2 = 20$, which is greater than 19, the correct answer is A. The two equations could be solved for x and y, giving $x = 6$ and $y = 4$, and then $x^2 - y^2$ could be computed, but this solution is more time-consuming.

Column A	Column B
18. The area of an equilateral triangle with side 6	The area of a right triangle with legs $\sqrt{3}$ and 9

The area of a triangle is one half the product of the lengths of the base and the altitude. In column A, the length of the altitude must first be determined. A sketch of the triangle may be helpful.

The altitude h divides the base of an equilateral triangle into two equal parts. From the Pythagorean theorem, $h^2 + 3^2 = 6^2$ or $h = 3\sqrt{3}$. Therefore the area of the triangle in column A is $\frac{1}{2} \cdot 6 \cdot 3\sqrt{3} = 9\sqrt{3}$. In column B, the base and the altitude of the right triangle are the two legs, and therefore the area is $\frac{9\sqrt{3}}{2}$. Since $9\sqrt{3}$ is greater than $\frac{9\sqrt{3}}{2}$, the correct answer is A.

A point (x,y) is in region III.

Column A	Column B
19. x	y

From the fact that point (x,y) is in region III, it is clear that x and y are both negative. However, since the location of the point within the region is not known, the relative sizes of x and y cannot be determined; for example, if the point is $(-3, -6)$, $x > y$ but if the point is $(-6, -3)$, $x < y$. Thus the answer is D.

$$(273 \times 87) + q = 29,235$$
$$(273 \times 87) + p = 30,063$$

Column A	Column B
20. p	q

It is not necessary to do a lot of computation to solve this problem. The sum of a number and q is less than the sum of the same number and p. Therefore $q < p$, and the answer is A.

$$x^2 = y^2 + 1$$

Column A	Column B
21. x	y

From the given equation, it can be determined that $x^2 > y^2$; however, the relative sizes of x and y cannot be determined. For example, if $y = 0$, x could be 1 or -1 and, since there is no way to tell which number x is, the answer is D.

13

◼️ DISCRETE QUANTITATIVE ◼️

Each discrete question contains all the information needed for answering the question except for the basic mathematical knowledge assumed to be common to the backgrounds of all examinees. Many of these questions require little more than manipulation and very basic knowledge; others require the examinee to read, understand, and solve a problem that involves either an actual or an abstract situation.

The following strategies might be helpful in answering discrete quantitative questions.

◼️ Read each question carefully to determine what information is given and what is being asked.

◼️ Before attempting to answer a question, scan the answer choices; otherwise you may waste time putting answers in a form that is not given (for example, putting an answer in the form $\frac{\sqrt{2}}{2}$ when the options are given in the form $\frac{1}{\sqrt{2}}$ or finding the answer in decimal form, such as 0.25, when the choices are given in fractional form, such as $\frac{1}{4}$).

◼️ For questions that require approximations, scan the answer choices to get some idea of the required closeness of approximation; otherwise, you may waste time on long computations when a short mental process would be sufficient (for example, finding 48 percent of a number when taking half of the number would give a close enough approximation).

Directions for discrete quantitative questions and some examples with explanations follow.

Directions: **Each of the following questions has five answer choices. For each of these questions, select the best of the answer choices given.**

22. **The average of x and y is 20. If z = 5, what is the average of x, y, and z?**

    (A) $8\frac{1}{3}$ (B) 10 (C) $12\frac{1}{2}$ (D) 15 (E) $17\frac{1}{2}$

Since the average of x and y is 20, $\frac{x+y}{2} = 20$ or $x + y = 40$. Thus $x + y + z = x + y + 5 = 40 + 5 = 45$ and therefore $\frac{x+y+z}{3} = \frac{45}{3} = 15$. The correct answer is D.

23. **Several years ago, Minnesota produced $\frac{2}{3}$ and Michigan $\frac{1}{6}$ of all the iron ore produced in the United States. If all the other states combined produced 18 million tons in a year, how many million tons did Minnesota produce that year?**

    (A) 27 (B) 36 (C) 54 (D) 72 (E) 162

Since Minnesota produced $\frac{2}{3}$ and Michigan $\frac{1}{6}$ of all the iron ore produced in the United States, the two states together produced $\frac{5}{6}$ of the iron ore. Therefore the 18 million tons produced by the rest of the United States was $\frac{1}{6}$ of the total

production. Thus the total United States production was $6 \cdot 18 = 108$ million tons, and Minnesota produced $\frac{2}{3}(108) = 72$ million tons. The correct answer is D.

24. **Into how many segments, each 20 centimeters long, can a segment 5 meters long be divided? (1 meter = 100 centimeters)**

    (A) 20 (B) 25 (C) 45 (D) 50 (E) 80

Using the given information that there are 100 centimeters in a meter, it can be determined that there are 500 centimeters in 5 meters. The number of segments, each 20 centimeters long, into which a 500-centimeter segment can be divided is $\frac{500}{20} = 25$. The answer is B.

25. **If $\frac{x}{3} - \frac{x}{6} + \frac{x}{9} - \frac{x}{12} = 1 - \frac{1}{2} + \frac{1}{3} - \frac{1}{4}$, then x =**

    (A) 3 (B) 1 (C) $\frac{1}{3}$ (D) $-\frac{1}{3}$ (E) -3

This problem can be solved without a lot of computation by factoring $\frac{x}{3}$ out of the expression on the left side of the equation $\frac{x}{3} - \frac{x}{6} + \frac{x}{9} - \frac{x}{12} = \frac{x}{3}(1 - \frac{1}{2} + \frac{1}{3} - \frac{1}{4})$ and substituting the factored expression into the equation, obtaining $\frac{x}{3}(1 - \frac{1}{2} + \frac{1}{3} - \frac{1}{4}) = 1 - \frac{1}{2} + \frac{1}{3} - \frac{1}{4}$. Dividing both sides of the equation by $1 - \frac{1}{2} + \frac{1}{3} - \frac{1}{4}$ (which is not zero) gives the resulting equation, $\frac{x}{3} = 1$. Thus $x = 3$ and the answer is A.

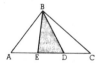

26. **In the figure above, if AE = ED = DC and the area of the shaded region is 5, what is the area of △ABC?**

    (A) 10 (B) 12.5 (C) 15 (D) 20 (E) 25

In this geometry problem, the shaded triangular region has a base that is $\frac{1}{3}$ the base of △ABC and has the same height as △ABC. Therefore, the area of the shaded region is $\frac{1}{3}$ the area of △ABC, and hence the area of △ABC = 3(5) = 15. The answer is C.

27. **Joan earned twice as much as Bill and Sam earned $3 more than half as much as Bill. If the amounts earned by Joan, Bill, and Sam are j, b, and s, respectively, which of the following is a correct ordering of these amounts?**

    (A) j < b < s (B) j < s < b
    (C) b < j < s (D) b < s < j
    (E) It cannot be determined from the information given.

From the first sentence the following two equations can be written: $j = 2b$ and $s = \frac{1}{2}b + 3$. The first equation implies that j is greater than b (j > b). The second equation, however, does not imply anything about the relationship between s and b; for example, if b = 2, s = $\frac{1}{2}$ (2) + 3 = 4 and s > b but if b = 8, s = $\frac{1}{2}$ (8) + 3 = 7 and s < b. Thus E is the best of the choices given.

■DATA INTERPRETATION■

The data interpretation questions, like the reading comprehension questions in the verbal measure, usually appear in sets. These questions are based on data presented in tables or graphs and test one's ability to synthesize information, to select appropriate data for answering a question, or to determine that sufficient information for answering a question is not provided.

The following strategies might help in answering sets of data interpretation questions.

■ Scan the set of data briefly to see what it is about, but do not attempt to grasp everything before reading the first question. Become familiar with it gradually, while trying to answer the questions. Be sure to read all notes related to the data.

■ If a graph has insufficient grid lines, use the edge of the answer sheet as a grid line to help read more accurately.

■ When possible, try to determine averages by visualizing a line through the important values and estimating the midpoint rather than reading off each value and then computing the average. Remember the average must be somewhere between the least value and the greatest value.

■ If a question is too long and involved to take in at one time, break it down into parts and substitute the values from the graph for each part. Then reread the question and attempt to answer it.

■ If the numbers are large, estimate products and quotients instead of performing involved computations.

■ Remember that these questions are to be answered only on the basis of the data given, everyday facts (such as the number of days in a year), and your knowledge of mathematics. Do not make use of specific information that you recall that may seem to relate to the particular situation on which the questions are based unless that information is derivable from the data provided.

The directions for data interpretation questions are the same as those for the discrete questions. Some examples of data interpretation questions with explanations follow.

Questions 28-30 refer to the following table:

PERCENT CHANGE IN DOLLAR AMOUNT OF SALES IN CERTAIN RETAIL STORES FROM 1977 TO 1979

| | Percent Change | |
Store	From 1977 to 1978	From 1978 to 1979
P	+10	−10
Q	−20	+9
R	+5	+12
S	−7	−15
T	+17	−8

28. In 1979 which of the stores had greater sales than any of the others shown?

(A) P (B) Q (C) R (D) S
(E) It cannot be determined from the information given.

Since the only information given in the table is the percent change from year to year, there is no way to compare the amount of sales for the stores in any one year. The best answer is E.

29. In store T, the sales for 1978 amounted to approximately what percent of the sales for 1979?

(A) 86% (B) 92% (C) 109% (D) 117% (E) 122%

If A is the amount of sales for store T in 1978, then 0.08 A is the amount of decrease and A − 0.08 A = 0.92 A is the amount of sales for 1979. Therefore the desired result can be obtained by dividing A by 0.92 A, which equals $\frac{1}{0.92}$ or approximately 109%. The best answer is C.

30. If sales in store P amounted to $800,000 in 1977, what did the sales amount to in that store in 1979?

(A) $727,200 (B) $792,000 (C) $800,000
(D) $880,000 (E) $968,000

If sales in store P amounted to $800,000 in 1977, then in 1978 they amounted to 110 percent of that; i.e., $880,000. In 1979 sales amounted to 90 percent of $880,000; i.e., $792,000. Note that an increase of 10 percent in one year and a decrease of 10 percent in the following year does not result in the same amount as the original amount of sales because the base used in computing the percents changes from $800,000 to $880,000. The correct answer is B.

Questions 31-34 refer to the following data.

World Crude Oil Production
(billions of barrels)

Revenues from Oil Exports
(billions of dollars)

	1973	1974	1975
Saudi Arabia	5.2	27.5	26.8
Iran	4.1	18.6	19.2
Iraq	1.5	6.0	8.3
Venezuela	3.3	10.3	8.2
Kuwait	2.0	8.3	7.8
United Arab Emirates	0.9	4.1	6.4
Nigeria	2.0	8.1	6.4
Libya	2.3	6.8	5.8
Indonesia	0.9	3.9	4.3
Algeria	1.3	4.1	3.4
Total	23.5	97.7	96.6

(1 billion = 1,000,000,000)

Note: Drawn to scale.

31. How many of the countries shown produced more crude oil in 1975 than in 1974?

(A) None (B) One (C) Two
(D) Three (E) Four

To answer this question, one needs only to examine the bar graph that deals with production and count the number of countries for which the solid bar is taller than the lined bar. The Soviet Union and Iraq are the only such countries; therefore, the answer is C.

32. In 1974, for which of the following countries were revenues from oil exports most nearly equal to 20 percent of the total for all the countries listed?

(A) Iran (B) Iraq (C) Kuwait
(D) Saudi Arabia (E) Venezuela

For this question, only the table is needed. Since 20 percent of the total (97.7) is a little less than 20, and 18.6, the revenue for Iran, is the only 1974 entry that is a little less than 20, the answer is A.

33. The country that had the greatest percent decrease in crude oil production from 1974 to 1975 had how many billions of dollars of revenue from oil exports in 1974?

(A) $27.5 (B) $18.6 (C) $10.3 (D) $8.1 (E) $4.1

This question requires the use of both the bar graph and the table. From the bar graph, it can be seen that there are seven countries that had a decrease in production; however, it would be very time-consuming to compute all of the percents. If the percent decrease is to be the greatest, then the difference between the two bars must be larger in relation to the height of the lined bar than any of the others. Some countries, such as the United States and United Arab Emirates, can be ruled out because the heights of the bars are so nearly the same. Venezuela and Kuwait can be ruled out because they have smaller differences but taller lined bars than Nigeria. Iran can be ruled out because it has about the same difference as Nigeria but a much taller lined bar. That leaves only Saudi Arabia and Nigeria and one would suspect that the ratio of the difference to the height of the lined bar is smaller for Saudi Arabia. A quick check shows that $\frac{0.5}{3}$ is less than $\frac{0.2}{0.9}$ and, therefore, Nigeria had the greatest percent decrease. From the table, Nigeria had 8.1 billions of dollars of revenue, and the best answer is D.

34. Which of the following can be concluded from the data?

I. In 1974, Iraq exported four times as many barrels of oil as in 1973.
II. In 1974, Iran exported three times as much oil as Iraq.
III. In 1975, the combined crude oil production of the Soviet Union, the United States, and Saudi Arabia was more than half of the total production of all nine countries shown.

(A) I only (B) II only (C) III only
(D) I and II (E) II and III

In this question, you have to decide whether each of three statements can be concluded from the data. Statement I cannot be concluded since no information is given about numbers of barrels exported in either year or about revenue per barrel in any given year. Although Iran's revenue in 1974 was approximately three times that of Iraq, no information is given about the cost per barrel in each of the countries; therefore, Statement II cannot be concluded. Note that it cannot be assumed that the price per barrel is the same in Iran and Iraq (although it might seem to be a reasonable assumption on the basis of outside knowledge) because no such information is provided in the data. In 1975 the combined production of the Soviet Union, the United States, and Saudi Arabia was about 9 billion barrels. Iran's production was about 2 billion and the remaining 5 countries produced

less than 1 billion each, giving a total of less than 7 billion barrels for these countries. Therefore Statement III can be concluded, and the answer is C.

Analytical Ability

Each analytical section includes two kinds of questions:

- analytical reasoning questions in groups of three or more questions, with each group based on a different set of conditions describing a fictional situation, and

- logical reasoning questions, usually with each question based on a separate short prose passage, but sometimes with two or three questions based on the same passage.

These sections of the General Test are designed to measure the ability to think analytically. Analytical reasoning questions focus on the ability to analyze a given structure of arbitrary relationships and to deduce new information from that structure, and logical reasoning questions focus on the ability to understand and to analyze relationships among arguments or parts of an argument.

The directions for all the questions in the analytical ability sections are the same and are as follows:

Directions: **Each question or group of questions is based on a passage or set of conditions. In answering some of the questions, it may be useful to draw a rough diagram. For each question, select the best answer choice given.**

ANALYTICAL REASONING

Analytical reasoning questions test the ability to understand a given structure of arbitrary relationships among fictitious persons, places, things, or events; to deduce new information from the relationships given; and to assess the conditions used to establish the structure of relationships. Each analytical reasoning group consists of (1) a set of about three to seven related statements or conditions (and sometimes other explanatory material) describing a structure of relationships, and (2) three or more questions that test understanding of that structure and its implications. Although each question in a group is based on the same set of conditions, the questions are independent of one another; answering one question in a group does not depend on answering any other question.

No knowledge of formal logic or mathematics is required for solving analytical reasoning problems. Although some of the same processes of reasoning are involved in solving both analytical reasoning problems and problems in those specialized fields, analytical reasoning problems can be solved using knowledge, skills, vocabulary, and computational ability (simple addition and subtraction) common to college students.

Each group of analytical reasoning questions is based on a set of conditions that establish relationships among persons, places, things, or events. These relationships are common ones such as temporal order (X arrived before Y but after Z), spatial order (City X is west of point Y and point Z), set membership (If Professor Green serves on the committee, then Professor Brown must also serve), cause and effect (Event Q always causes event R), and family relationship (Mary is Juan's mother and Belinda's sister-in-law). The conditions should be read carefully to determine the exact nature of the relationship or relationships involved. Some relationships are fixed or constant (The second house on the block belongs to P). Other relationships are variable (Q must be assigned to either campsite 1 or campsite 3). Some relationships that are not given can be easily deduced from those given. (If one condition about books on a shelf specifies that book L is to the left of book Y, and another specifies that book P is to the left of book L, then it can be deduced that book P is to the left of book Y.)

The following strategies may be helpful in answering analytical reasoning questions:

- In general, it is best to answer first those questions in a group that seem to pose little difficulty and then to return to those that seem troublesome. It is best not to start one group before finishing another because much time can be lost later in returning to an analytical reasoning group and reestablishing familiarity with its relationships. Do not avoid a group merely because its conditions look long or complicated.

- In reading the conditions, it is important not to introduce unwarranted assumptions; for instance, in a set establishing relationships of height and weight among the members of a team, do not assume that a person who is taller than another person must weigh more than that person.

- Since it is intended that the conditions be as clear as possible, avoid interpreting them as if they were designed to trick you by means of hidden ambiguities or other such devices. When in doubt, read the conditions in their most obvious, common-language sense. This does not mean, however, that the language in the conditions is not intended to be read for precise meaning. It is essential, for instance, to pay particular attention to function words that describe or limit relationships, such as *only, exactly, never, always, must be, cannot be,* and the like. The result of the thorough reading described above should be a clear picture of a structure of relationships, including what kind or kinds of relationships are involved, who or what the participants in the relationships are, and what is and is not known about the structure of the relationships. For instance, at this point it can often be determined whether only a single configuration of relationships is permitted by the conditions or whether alternatives are permitted.

- Many examinees find it useful to underline key points in the conditions or to draw a simple diagram, as the directions for the analytical sections suggest.

- Even though some people who solve analytical reasoning problems find diagrams to be helpful, other people seldom resort to them. And among those who do regularly use diagrams, there is by no means universal agreement on which kind of diagram is best for which problem or in which cases a diagram is most useful. Therefore, do not be concerned if a particular problem in the test seems to be best approached without the use of diagrams.

- Each question should be considered separately from the other questions in its group; no information, except what is given in the original conditions, should be carried over from one question to another. In many cases a question will simply ask for conclusions to be drawn from the conditions as originally given. An individual question can, however, add information to the original conditions or temporarily suspend one of the original conditions for the purpose of that question only.

SAMPLE QUESTIONS WITH EXPLANATIONS

Questions 35-36

A half tone is the smallest possible interval between notes.
Note T is a half tone higher than note V.
Note V is a whole tone higher than note W.
Note W is a half tone lower than note X.
Note X is a whole tone lower than note T.
Note Y is a whole tone lower than note W.

35. Which of the following represents the relative order of the notes from the lowest to the highest?

   (A) X Y W V T   (B) Y W X V T   (C) W V T Y X
   (D) Y W V T X   (E) Y X W V T

The answer to this question can be determined by reading the six given statements and understanding the relationships among them. The relationships may be clarified by drawing a simple illustrative diagram:

T
V
X
W

Y

The diagram shows the relative order of the notes; since the question asks for the order from the lowest note to the highest, the correct answer is (B).

36. Which of the following statements about an additional note, Z, could NOT be true?

   (A) Z is higher than T.   (B) Z is lower than Y.
   (C) Z is lower than W.   (D) Z is between W and Y.
   (E) Z is between W and X.

Since W and X are a half tone apart, and since a half tone is the smallest possible interval between notes, Z cannot be between W and X. The best answer is therefore (E).

Questions 37-39

F, H, I, J, K, L, M, and N spoke, but not necessarily in that order. Only one person spoke at a time.
F spoke after L and took more time than H.
I spoke before M and after H, and took less time than K.
J spoke after N and before H, and took less time than N and more time than K.
N spoke after F and took less time than H.

37. Of the following, which spoke first?

   (A) H   (B) I   (C) J   (D) L   (E) N

38. Of the following, which took the most time?

   (A) F   (B) H   (C) J   (D) K   (E) N

39. Which of the following must be true?

   (A) F was the second speaker and gave the third lengthiest speech.
   (B) H spoke before I and took more time than N.
   (C) I spoke last and gave the shortest speech.
   (D) J spoke after M and took less time than F.
   (E) N spoke after L and took more time than F.

These questions may be answered by making two lists of the speakers, as follows:

Order of appearance: L F N J H I M
Length of speech: F H N J K I

From these two lists the answers to all three questions emerge. The answer to 37 is (D), to 38 (A), and to 39 (B). For question 39, it is necessary to note that although (A) could be true, there is insufficient information provided to establish that it must be true.

Questions 40-42

To apply to college a student must see the school counselor, obtain a transcript at the transcript office, and obtain a recommendation from Teacher A or Teacher B.
A student must see the counselor before obtaining a transcript.
The counselor is available only Friday mornings and Tuesday, Wednesday, and Thursday afternoons.
The transcript office is open only Tuesday and Wednesday mornings, Thursday afternoons, and Friday mornings.
Teacher A is available only Monday and Wednesday mornings.
Teacher B is available only Monday afternoons and Friday mornings.

40. A student has already seen the counselor and does not care from which teacher she obtains her recommendation. Which of the following is a complete and accurate list of those days when she could possibly complete the application process in one day?

    (A) Friday   (B) Monday, Wednesday
    (C) Monday, Friday   (D) Wednesday, Friday
    (E) Monday, Wednesday, Friday

To complete the application process in one day, the student has to obtain a transcript and a recommendation on the same day. This will be possible on Wednesdays, when both the transcript office and teacher A are accessible, and on Fridays, when both the transcript office and teacher B are accessible, and at no other time. The only other day that a teacher recommendation can be obtained is Monday, but on Mondays no transcripts can be obtained. Thus, the correct answer is (D).

41. A student completed his application procedure in one day. Which of the following statements must be true?

    I. He obtained his recommendation from Teacher A.
    II. He obtained his recommendation from Teacher B.
    III. He completed the procedure in the morning.

    (A) I only   (B) II only   (C) III only
    (D) I and III only   (E) II and III only

If a student completed the entire application procedure in a single day, that day must have been a Friday. It could not have been a Monday, since on Mondays neither counselor nor transcript office is accessible. It could not have been either a Tuesday or a Thursday, because on neither of these days would a teacher have been available for a recommendation. And it could not have been a Wednesday because on Wednesdays one cannot see the counselor before obtaining a transcript. Now, given that the student in question must have done everything on a Friday, I must be false since teacher A is not available on Fridays, II must be true since teacher B is both available on Fridays and the only teacher to be so

available, and III must also be true since on Fridays all of the relevant business can only be conducted in the morning. Therefore, the correct answer is (E).

42. A student has already obtained his transcript and does not care from which teacher he obtains his recommendation. Which of the following is a complete and accurate list of those days when he could possibly complete the application process?

    (A) Friday   (B) Monday, Wednesday
    (C) Monday, Friday   (D) Wednesday, Friday
    (E) Monday, Wednesday, Friday

If the student has already obtained his transcript, he must have seen the counselor, too, since seeing the counselor must precede receipt of a transcript. This means that obtaining a recommendation from a teacher is all that is left to do. Since it does not matter which teacher the recommendation is from, the application process can be completed on any day that either teacher A or teacher B is available. Those days are Monday, when both are available, Wednesday, when A is available, and Friday, when B is available. The correct answer, therefore, is (E).

Questions 43-44

A farmer plants only five different kinds of vegetables—beans, corn, kale, peas, and squash. Every year the farmer plants exactly three kinds of vegetables according to the following restrictions:

If the farmer plants corn, he also plants beans that year.
If the farmer plants kale one year, he does not plant it the next year.
In any year, the farmer plants no more than one of the vegetables he planted in the previous year.

43. Which of the following is a possible sequence of combinations for the farmer to plant in two successive years?

    (A) Beans, corn, kale; corn, peas, squash
    (B) Beans, corn, peas; beans, corn, squash
    (C) Beans, peas, squash; beans, corn, kale
    (D) Corn, peas, squash; beans, kale, peas
    (E) Kale, peas, squash; beans, corn, kale

Options (A) and (D) are not possible because corn appears as a vegetable without beans in a given year. Option (E) is not possible because kale appears in two successive years. Option (B) is not possible because two vegetables are repeated in two successive years. Option (C) contains a possible sequence of combinations.

44. If the farmer plants beans, corn, and kale in the first year, which of the following combinations must be planted in the third year?

    (A) Beans, corn, and kale
    (B) Beans, corn, and peas
    (C) Beans, kale, and peas
    (D) Beans, peas, and squash
    (E) Kale, peas, and squash

Beans, peas, and squash are planted in the second year, since kale may not be repeated two consecutive years and since corn cannot be repeated without repeating beans (only one vegetable can be repeated in consecutive years). In the third year, corn and kale must be planted (only one of the second year vegetables may be repeated). Beans are planted whenever corn is planted, so (A) is the correct answer choice.

Logical reasoning questions test the ability to understand, analyze, and evaluate arguments. Some of the abilities tested by specific questions include recognizing the point of an argument, recognizing assumptions on which an argument is based, drawing conclusions from given premises, inferring material missing from given passages, applying principles governing one argument to another, identifying methods of argument, evaluating arguments and counterarguments, and analyzing evidence.

Each question or group of questions is based on a short argument, generally an excerpt from the kind of material graduate students are likely to encounter in their academic and personal reading. Although arguments may be drawn from specific fields of study such as philosophy, literary criticism, social studies, and the physical sciences, materials from more familiar sources such as political speeches, advertisements, and informal discussions or dialogues also form the basis for some questions. No specialized knowledge of any particular field is required for answering the questions, however, and no knowledge of the terminology of formal logic is presupposed.

Specific questions asked about the arguments draw on information obtained by the process of critical and analytical reading described above.

The following strategies may be helpful in answering logical reasoning questions:

■ The passage on which a question (or questions) is based should be read very carefully with close attention to such matters as (1) what is said specifically about a subject, (2) what is not said but necessarily follows from what is said, (3) what is suggested or claimed without substantiation in what is said. In addition, the means of relating statements, inferences, and claims—the structure of the argument—should be noted. Such careful reading may lead to the conclusion that the argument presented proceeds in an unsound or illogical fashion, but in many cases there will be no apparent weakness in the argument. It is important, in reading the arguments given, to attend to the soundness of the method employed and not to the actual truth of opinions presented.

■ It is important to determine exactly what information the question is asking for; for instance, although it might be expected that one would be asked to detect or name the most glaring fault in a weak argument, the question posed may actually ask for the selection of one of a group of other arguments that reveals the same fault. In some cases, questions may ask for a negative response, for instance, a weakness that is NOT found in an argument or a conclusion that CANNOT be drawn from an argument.

45. If Ramón was born in New York State, then he is a citizen of the United States.

The statement above can be deduced logically from which of the following statements?

(A) Everyone born in New York State is a citizen of the United States.
(B) Every citizen of the United States is a resident either of one of the states or of one of the territories.
(C) Some people born in New York State are citizens of the United States.
(D) Ramón was born either in New York or in Florida.
(E) Ramón is a citizen either of the United States or of the Dominican Republic.

The question here is which of (A) through (E), if true, would guarantee that Ramón cannot have his birthplace in New York State without being a United States citizen. Since, crucially, the relationship between birthplace and citizenship is at stake, any statement that concerns itself with birthplace alone, like (D), or citizenship alone, like (E), or with the relationship between residence and citizenship, like (B), will be unsuitable for providing any such guarantee. This leaves (A) and (C), both of which deal with the relationship at issue here. Of these, (C) makes the weaker claim: It leaves open the possibility that there might be people born in New York State who are not United States citizens, and it leaves open whether or not Ramón is one of those people. (A), on the other hand, rules out any possibility of anyone being born in New York State and yet not being a United States citizen. Therefore, (A) rules out that possibility for Ramón also, and (A) is thus the correct answer.

46. There is no reason to rule out the possibility of life on Uranus. We must, then, undertake the exploration of that planet.

The argument above assumes that

(A) life exists on Uranus
(B) Uranus is the only other planet in the solar system capable of supporting life
(C) Uranian life would be readily recognizable as life
(D) the search for life is a sufficient motive for space exploration
(E) no one has previously proposed the exploration of Uranus

The argument is based on the weak claim that there is a possibility that life may exist on Uranus and not on the stronger claim that life on Uranus actually exists; since logically weak claims do not presuppose logically stronger claims, (A) is not an assumption. (B) is likewise readily eliminated since the author's argument is presented as independent of any comparison of Uranus with other planets. (E) is also clearly not the correct answer: There is no hint in the argument that its author takes it to be a novel one or takes its conclusion to be a novel one. (C) comes closer to being an assumption of the argument: If the mere possibility of the existence of life on Uranus is taken as an impetus for exploration, we can safely conclude that a major aim of any such exploration would be to ascertain whether or not actually was life on Uranus. But this search for life does not presuppose that the techniques scientists on earth have for detecting life will be adequate for recognizing possibly alien life forms in every case. Even less is it presupposed that this task will be relatively easy. So (C) cannot be an assumption of the argument. The correct answer is (D), for, if (D) is true, the mere possibility of there being life on Uranus is indeed a compelling reason for the exploration of the planet.

47. The rush to use distilled grains as petroleum substitutes poses potential market problems. By 1985, the value of corn as alcohol will exceed the value of corn as food. Alcohol produced from grain will displace some imported oil, and the price of oil will begin to dictate the price of corn.

    If the claims made in the passage above are true, which of the following draws the most reliable inference about the effect of a reduction in the price of imported oil after 1985?

    (A) Some corn would be diverted from energy markets into food markets.
    (B) A downward pressure would be exerted on the price of corn.
    (C) An upward pressure would be exerted on the world-wide demand for corn.
    (D) Farmers would have an incentive to grow more corn.
    (E) Energy companies would have an incentive to produce more domestic oil.

If the price of oil is beginning to dictate the price of corn, then one would expect that a decrease in the price of imported oil will exert some downward pressure on the price of corn. This much can reliably be inferred, and (B) is, therefore the correct answer. None of (A), (C), (D), or (E) can be inferred with a similar degree of confidence. (A) could perhaps be inferred if, as a result of the decrease in the price of imported oil, the value of corn as food once more exceeded the price of corn as alcohol; but we lack any information on this point. The worldwide demand for corn might increase if corn as alcohol proved to be a relatively inexpensive alternative to oil; but a drop in the price of oil makes oil more, not less, price-competitive, so (C) cannot be inferred. (D) might be inferred if corn prices could be expected to rise; but corn prices are liable to fall, so (D) cannot be inferred. (E) might be inferred if the price of imported oil had increased; but we are considering a situation in which the price of imported oil is reduced, so (E) cannot be inferred.

48. Offshore blasting in oil exploration does not hurt fishing; blasting started this year, and this year's salmon catch has been the largest in a long time.

    All of the following statements, if true, are valid objections to the argument above EXCEPT:

    (A) The salmon is only one of many species of fish that might be affected by the blasts.
    (B) The rapid changes of water pressure caused by the blasts make salmon mate more frequently.
    (C) The noise of the blasts interferes with the food chain salmon depend on.
    (D) Factors that have nothing to do with the well-being of salmon may significantly affect the size of one year's catch.
    (E) Vibrations from the blasts destroy fish eggs.

The given argument draws a general conclusion on the basis of a seemingly relevant particular observation. The question takes for granted that the general conclusion drawn is not adequately supported by the evidence cited and asks for a discrimination between the kinds of factual observations that would actually show the argument to be flawed and the kinds of factual observations that would not do so. (A) points out that some other kinds of fish may be hurt even if salmon are not. (D) points out that the size of the catch depends on other factors, like the number of fishermen trying to catch fish. (C) and (E) both revolve around the fact that the argument seems to assume that any effects of offshore blasting would have immediate impact on fishing; both point out facts that are reasonably construed as implying negative effects of the blasts in the long run. (B), on the other hand, is most naturally construed as suggesting that the salmon population may well increase, which in turn should help fishing rather than hurt it. So (B) is most readily interpreted as making the conclusion of the argument more likely to be true. Since no statement that supports the conclusion of an argument will, under ordinary circumstances, constitute a valid objection to that argument, (B) is the correct answer.

THE GRADUATE RECORD EXAMINATIONS

General Test

SECTION 1

Time—30 minutes

38 Questions

Directions: Each sentence below has one or two blanks, each blank indicating that something has been omitted. Beneath the sentence are five lettered words or sets of words. Choose the word or set of words for each blank that best fits the meaning of the sentence as a whole.

1. Clearly refuting sceptics, researchers have ------- not only that gravitational radiation exists but that it also does exactly what theory ------- it should do.

   (A) doubted. .warranted
   (B) estimated. .accepted
   (C) demonstrated. .predicted
   (D) assumed. .deduced
   (E) supposed. .asserted

2. Sponsors of the bill were ------- because there was no opposition to it within the legislature until after the measure had been signed into law.

   (A) unreliable   (B) well-intentioned
   (C) persistent   (D) relieved   (E) detained

3. The paradoxical aspect of the myths about Demeter, when we consider the predominant image of her as a tranquil and serene goddess, is her ------- search for her daughter.

   (A) extended
   (B) agitated
   (C) comprehensive
   (D) motiveless
   (E) heartless

4. Yellow fever, the disease that killed 4,000 Philadelphians in 1793, and so ------- Memphis, Tennessee, that the city lost its charter, has reappeared after nearly two decades in ------- in the Western Hemisphere.

   (A) terrorized. .contention
   (B) ravaged. .secret
   (C) disabled. .quarantine
   (D) corrupted. .quiescence
   (E) decimated. .abeyance

5. Although -------, almost self-effacing in his private life, he displays in his plays and essays a strong ------- publicity and controversy.

   (A) conventional. .interest in
   (B) monotonous. .reliance on
   (C) shy. .aversion toward
   (D) retiring. .penchant for
   (E) evasive. .impatience with

6. Comparatively few rock musicians are willing to laugh at themselves, although a hint of ------- can boost sales of video clips very nicely.

   (A) self-deprecation
   (B) congeniality
   (C) cynicism
   (D) embarrassment
   (E) self-doubt

7. Parts of seventeenth-century Chinese pleasure gardens were not necessarily intended to look -------; they were designed expressly to evoke the agreeable melancholy resulting from a sense of the ------- of natural beauty and human glory.

   (A) beautiful. .immutability
   (B) cheerful. .transitoriness
   (C) colorful. .abstractness
   (D) luxuriant. .simplicity
   (E) conventional. .wildness

GO ON TO THE NEXT PAGE.

Directions: In each of the following questions, a related pair of words or phrases is followed by five lettered pairs of words or phrases. Select the lettered pair that best expresses a relationship similar to that expressed in the original pair.

8. APPLE : SKIN :: (A) potato : tuber
   (B) melon : rind   (C) tomato : fruit
   (D) maize : cob   (E) rhubarb : leafstalk

9. FIRE : INFERNO ::
   (A) speech : shout
   (B) wind : temperature
   (C) storm : hurricane
   (D) whale : minnow
   (E) plant : flower

10. BODYGUARD : PERSON ::
    (A) police officer : traffic   (B) teacher : pupil
    (C) mayor : city   (D) soldier : country
    (E) secretary : office

11. LOPE : RUN :: (A) uncover : lose
    (B) view : see   (C) sigh : moan
    (D) chew : drink   (E) drawl : speak

12. HOAX : DECEIVE ::
    (A) scandal : vilify
    (B) lottery : disburse
    (C) gimmick : wheedle
    (D) filibuster : delay
    (E) boast : cajole

13. ALCOVE : RECESS ::
    (A) turret : chimney   (B) dome : roof
    (C) column : entrance   (D) foyer : ballroom
    (E) foundation : building

14. BALLAST : INSTABILITY ::
    (A) buoy : direction   (B) purchase : slippage
    (C) lathe : metal   (D) pulley : leverage
    (E) hoist : elevator

15. MUFFLE : SOUND :: (A) assuage : grief
    (B) maul : object   (C) extract : flavor
    (D) endure : agony   (E) conceal : secret

16. MITIGATE : SEVERE ::
    (A) compile : available
    (B) restore : new
    (C) contribute : charitable
    (D) venerate : reverent
    (E) qualify : general

GO ON TO THE NEXT PAGE.

Directions: Each passage in this group is followed by questions based on its content. After reading a passage, choose the best answer to each question. Answer all questions following a passage on the basis of what is stated or implied in that passage.

A Marxist sociologist has argued that racism stems from the class struggle that is unique to the capitalist system—that racial prejudice is generated by capitalists as a means of controlling workers. His thesis works relatively well when applied to discrimination against Blacks in the United States, but his definition of racial prejudice as "racially-based negative prejudgments against a group generally accepted as a race in any given region of ethnic competition," can be interpreted as also including hostility toward such ethnic groups as the Chinese in California and the Jews in medieval Europe. However, since prejudice against these latter peoples was not inspired by capitalists, he has to reason that such antagonisms were not really based on race. He disposes thusly (albeit unconvincingly) of both the intolerance faced by Jews before the rise of capitalism and the early twentieth-century discrimination against Oriental people in California, which, inconveniently, was instigated by workers.

17. The passage supplies information that would answer which of the following questions?

(A) What accounts for the prejudice against the Jews in medieval Europe?
(B) What conditions caused the discrimination against Oriental people in California in the early twentieth century?
(C) Which groups are not in ethnic competition with each other in the United States?
(D) What explanation did the Marxist sociologist give for the existence of racial prejudice?
(E) What evidence did the Marxist sociologist provide to support his thesis?

18. The author considers the Marxist sociologist's thesis about the origins of racial prejudice to be

(A) unoriginal
(B) unpersuasive
(C) offensive
(D) obscure
(E) speculative

19. It can be inferred from the passage that the Marxist sociologist would argue that in a noncapitalist society racial prejudice would be

(A) pervasive
(B) tolerated
(C) ignored
(D) forbidden
(E) nonexistent

20. According to the passage, the Marxist sociologist's chain of reasoning required him to assert that prejudice toward Oriental people in California was

(A) directed primarily against the Chinese
(B) similar in origin to prejudice against the Jews
(C) understood by Oriental people as ethnic competition
(D) provoked by workers
(E) nonracial in character

GO ON TO THE NEXT PAGE.

By 1950, the results of attempts to relate brain processes to mental experience appeared rather discouraging. Such variations in size, shape, chemistry, conduction speed, excitation threshold, and the
(5) like as had been demonstrated in nerve cells remained negligible in significance for any possible correlation with the manifold dimensions of mental experience.

Near the turn of the century, it had been sug-
(10) gested by Hering that different modes of sensation, such as pain, taste, and color, might be correlated with the discharge of specific kinds of nervous energy. However, subsequently developed methods of recording and analyzing nerve potentials failed
(15) to reveal any such qualitative diversity. It was possible to demonstrate by other methods refined structural differences among neuron types; however, proof was lacking that the quality of the impulse or its conduction was influenced by these differences,
(20) which seemed instead to influence the developmental patterning of the neural circuits. Although qualitative variance among nerve energies was never rigidly disproved, the doctrine was generally abandoned in favor of the opposing view, namely, that
(25) nerve impulses are essentially homogeneous in quality and are transmitted as "common currency" throughout the nervous system. According to this theory, it is not the quality of the sensory nerve impulses that determines the diverse conscious sen-
(30) sations they produce, but rather the different areas of the brain into which they discharge, and there is some evidence for this view. In one experiment, when an electric stimulus was applied to a given sensory field of the cerebral cortex of a conscious
(35) human subject, it produced a sensation of the appropriate modality for that particular locus, that is, a visual sensation from the visual cortex, an auditory sensation from the auditory cortex, and so on. Other experiments revealed slight variations in
(40) the size, number, arrangement, and interconnection of the nerve cells, but as far as psychoneural correlations were concerned, the obvious similarities of these sensory fields to each other seemed much more remarkable than any of the minute differ-
(45) ences.

However, cortical locus, in itself, turned out to have little explanatory value. Studies showed that sensations as diverse as those of red, black, green, and white, or touch, cold, warmth, movement,
(50) pain, posture, and pressure apparently may arise through activation of the same cortical areas. What seemed to remain was some kind of differential patterning effects in the brain excitation: it is the difference in the central distribution of impulses that
(55) counts. In short, brain theory suggested a correlation between mental experience and the activity of relatively homogeneous nerve-cell units conducting essentially homogeneous impulses through homogeneous cerebral tissue. To match the multiple dimen-
(60) sions of mental experience psychologists could only point to a limitless variation in the spatiotemporal patterning of nerve impulses.

21. The author suggests that, by 1950, attempts to correlate mental experience with brain processes would probably have been viewed with

(A) indignation   (B) impatience   (C) pessimism
(D) indifference   (E) defiance

22. The author mentions "common currency" in line 26 primarily in order to emphasize the

(A) lack of differentiation among nerve impulses in human beings
(B) similarity of the sensations that all human beings experience
(C) similarities in the views of scientists who have studied the human nervous system
(D) continuous passage of nerve impulses through the nervous system
(E) recurrent questioning by scientists of an accepted explanation about the nervous system

23. The description in lines 32-38 of an experiment in which electric stimuli were applied to different sensory fields of the cerebral cortex tends to support the theory that

(A) the simple presence of different cortical areas cannot account for the diversity of mental experience
(B) variation in spatiotemporal patterning of nerve impulses correlates with variation in subjective experience
(C) nerve impulses are essentially homogeneous and are relatively unaffected as they travel through the nervous system
(D) the mental experiences produced by sensory nerve impulses are determined by the cortical area activated
(E) variation in neuron types affects the quality of nerve impulses

GO ON TO THE NEXT PAGE.

24. According to the passage, some evidence exists that the area of the cortex activated by a sensory stimulus determines which of the following?

    I. The nature of the nerve impulse
    II. The modality of the sensory experience
    III. Qualitative differences within a modality

    (A) II only   (B) III only   (C) I and II only
    (D) II and III only   (E) I, II, and III

25. The passage can most accurately be described as a discussion concerning historical views of the

    (A) anatomy of the brain
    (B) manner in which nerve impulses are conducted
    (C) significance of different cortical areas in mental experience
    (D) mechanics of sense perception
    (E) physiological correlates of mental experience

26. Which of the following best summarizes the author's opinion of the suggestion that different areas of the brain determine perceptions produced by sensory nerve impulses?

    (A) It is a plausible explanation, but it has not been completely proved.
    (B) It is the best explanation of brain processes currently available.
    (C) It is disproved by the fact that the various areas of the brain are physiologically very similar.
    (D) There is some evidence to support it, but it fails to explain the diversity of mental experience.
    (E) There is experimental evidence that confirms its correctness.

27. It can be inferred from the passage that which of the following exhibit the LEAST qualitative variation?

    (A) Nerve cells
    (B) Nerve impulses
    (C) Cortical areas
    (D) Spatial patterns of nerve impulses
    (E) Temporal patterns of nerve impulses

GO ON TO THE NEXT PAGE.

Directions: Each question below consists of a word printed in capital letters, followed by five lettered words or phrases. Choose the lettered word or phrase that is most nearly opposite in meaning to the word in capital letters.

Since some of the questions require you to distinguish fine shades of meaning, be sure to consider all the choices before deciding which one is best.

28. LAG: (A) look around   (B) dodge easily
    (C) seem hard   (D) forge ahead
    (E) change radically

29. RANDOMIZE: (A) distribute   (B) analyze
    (C) systematize   (D) blend   (E) prepare

30. SURCHARGE: (A) loss   (B) liability
    (C) decrease   (D) shortfall   (E) discount

31. SYNCHRONOUS: (A) off-key
    (B) out-of-shape   (C) without pity
    (D) out-of-phase   (E) without difficulty

32. PROFUSE: (A) recurrent   (B) rare
    (C) comprehensible   (D) scanty   (E) flawed

33. INERTIA:
    (A) short duration
    (B) massless particle
    (C) resistant medium
    (D) ability to maintain pressure
    (E) tendency to change motion

34. DIN: (A) silence   (B) slowness
    (C) sharpness   (D) essence   (E) repose

35. GAUCHENESS: (A) probity   (B) sophistry
    (C) acumen   (D) polish   (E) vigor

36. INCHOATE: (A) sordid   (B) modern
    (C) improvised   (D) exceptionally quick
    (E) completely formed

37. ENDEMIC: (A) exotic   (B) shallow
    (C) episodic   (D) manifest   (E) treatable

38. REDOUBTABLE: (A) unsurprising
    (B) unambiguous   (C) unimpressive
    (D) inevitable   (E) immovable

S T O P

**IF YOU FINISH BEFORE TIME IS CALLED, YOU MAY CHECK YOUR WORK ON THIS SECTION ONLY.
DO NOT WORK ON ANY OTHER SECTION IN THE TEST.**

Section 2 starts on page 31.

SECTION 2

Time—30 minutes

38 Questions

Directions: Each sentence below has one or two blanks, each blank indicating that something has been omitted. Beneath the sentence are five lettered words or sets of words. Choose the word or set of words for each blank that best fits the meaning of the sentence as a whole.

1. Since it is now ------- to build the complex central processing unit of a computer on a single silicon chip using photolithography and chemical etching, it seems plausible that other miniature structures might be fabricated in ------- ways.

   (A) unprecedented. .undiscovered
   (B) difficult. .related
   (C) permitted. .unique
   (D) mandatory. .congruent
   (E) routine. .similar

2. Given the evidence of Egyptian and Babylonian ------- later Greek civilization, it would be incorrect to view the work of Greek scientists as an entirely independent creation.

   (A) disdain for
   (B) imitation of
   (C) ambivalence about
   (D) deference to
   (E) influence on

3. Laws do not ensure social order since laws can always be -------, which makes them ------- unless the authorities have the will and the power to detect and punish wrongdoing.

   (A) contested. .provisional
   (B) circumvented. .antiquated
   (C) repealed. .vulnerable
   (D) violated. .ineffective
   (E) modified. .unstable

4. Since she believed him to be both candid and trustworthy, she refused to consider the possibility that his statement had been -------.

   (A) irrelevant   (B) facetious   (C) mistaken
   (D) critical   (E) insincere

5. Ironically, the party leaders encountered no greater ------- their efforts to build a progressive party than the ------- of the progressives already elected to the legislature.

   (A) support for. .advocacy
   (B) threat to. .promise
   (C) benefit from. .success
   (D) obstacle to. .resistance
   (E) praise for. .reputation

6. It is strange how words shape our thoughts and trap us at the bottom of deeply ------- canyons of thinking, their imprisoning sides carved out by the ------- of past usage.

   (A) cleaved. .eruptions
   (B) rooted. .flood
   (C) incised. .river
   (D) ridged. .ocean
   (E) notched. .mountains

7. That his intransigence in making decisions ------- no open disagreement from any quarter was well known; thus, clever subordinates learned the art of ------- their opinions in casual remarks.

   (A) elicited. .quashing
   (B) engendered. .recasting
   (C) brooked. .intimating
   (D) embodied. .instigating
   (E) forbore. .emending

GO ON TO THE NEXT PAGE.

31

Directions: In each of the following questions, a related pair of words or phrases is followed by five lettered pairs of words or phrases. Select the lettered pair that best expresses a relationship similar to that expressed in the original pair.

8. BABBLE : TALK ::   (A) chisel : sculpt
   (B) harmonize : sing   (C) scribble : write
   (D) hint : imply   (E) quibble : elude

9. SYLLABUS : COURSE ::   (A) rules : jury
   (B) map : destination   (C) recipe : ingredients
   (D) appetizer : meal   (E) agenda : meeting

10. VARNISH : WOOD ::
    (A) etch : glass
    (B) tarnish : silver
    (C) wax : linoleum
    (D) burnish : metal
    (E) bleach : fabric

11. PITCH : SOUND ::   (A) color : light
    (B) mass : weight   (C) force : pressure
    (D) energy : heat   (E) velocity : time

12. DISCOMFITED : BLUSH ::
    (A) nonplussed : weep   (B) contemptuous : sneer
    (C) affronted : blink   (D) sullen : groan
    (E) aggrieved : gloat

13. INVINCIBLE : SUBDUED ::
    (A) inconsistent : expressed
    (B) impervious : damaged
    (C) imprudent : enacted
    (D) bolted : separated
    (E) expensive : bought

14. STRIATED : GROOVE ::
    (A) adorned : detail
    (B) woven : texture
    (C) engraved : curve
    (D) constructed : design
    (E) braided : strand

15. DOGGEREL : VERSE ::   (A) burlesque : play
    (B) sketch : drawing   (C) operetta : symphony
    (D) fable : narration   (E) limerick : sonnet

16. DROLL : LAUGH ::   (A) grisly : flinch
    (B) bland : tire   (C) shrill : shriek
    (D) coy : falter   (E) wily : smirk

GO ON TO THE NEXT PAGE.

Directions: Each passage in this group is followed by questions based on its content. After reading a passage, choose the best answer to each question. Answer all questions following a passage on the basis of what is stated or implied in that passage.

The transfer of heat and water vapor from the ocean to the air above it depends on a disequilibrium at the interface of the water and the air. Within about a millimeter of the water, air temperature is close to that of the surface water, and the air is nearly saturated with water vapor. But the differences, however small, are crucial, and the disequilibrium is maintained by air near the surface mixing with air higher up, which is typically appreciably cooler and lower in water-vapor content. The air is mixed by means of turbulence that depends on the wind for its energy. As wind speed increases, so does turbulence, and thus the rate of heat and moisture transfer. Detailed understanding of this phenomenon awaits further study. An interacting—and complicating—phenomenon is wind-to-water transfer of momentum that occurs when waves are formed. When the wind makes waves, it transfers important amounts of energy—energy that is therefore not available to provide turbulence.

17. The primary purpose of the passage is to

(A) resolve a controversy
(B) describe a phenomenon
(C) outline a theory
(D) confirm research findings
(E) classify various observations

18. According to the passage, wind over the ocean generally does which of the following?

I. Causes relatively cool, dry air to come into proximity with the ocean surface.
II. Maintains a steady rate of heat and moisture transfer between the ocean and the air.
III. Causes frequent changes in the temperature of the water at the ocean's surface.

(A) I only
(B) II only
(C) I and II only
(D) II and III only
(E) I, II, and III

19. It can be inferred from the passage that the author regards current knowledge about heat and moisture transfer from the ocean to air as

(A) revolutionary
(B) inconsequential
(C) outdated
(D) derivative
(E) incomplete

20. The passage suggests that if on a certain day the wind were to decrease until there was no wind at all, which of the following would occur?

(A) The air closest to the ocean surface would become saturated with water vapor.
(B) The air closest to the ocean surface would be warmer than the water.
(C) The amount of moisture in the air closest to the ocean surface would decrease.
(D) The rate of heat and moisture transfer would increase.
(E) The air closest to the ocean would be at the same temperature as air higher up.

GO ON TO THE NEXT PAGE.

Extraordinary creative activity has been characterized as revolutionary, flying in the face of what is established and producing not what is acceptable but what will become accepted. According to this formulation, highly creative activity transcends the limits of an existing form and establishes a new principle of organization. However, the idea that extraordinary creativity transcends established limits is misleading when it is applied to the arts, even though it may be valid for the sciences. Differences between highly creative art and highly creative science arise in part from a difference in their goals. For the sciences, a new theory is the goal and end result of the creative act. Innovative science produces new propositions in terms of which diverse phenomena can be related to one another in more coherent ways. Such phenomena as a brilliant diamond or a nesting bird are relegated to the role of data, serving as the means for formulating or testing a new theory. The goal of highly creative art is very different: the phenomenon itself becomes the direct product of the creative act. Shakespeare's *Hamlet* is not a tract about the behavior of indecisive princes or the uses of political power; nor is Picasso's painting *Guernica* primarily a propositional statement about the Spanish Civil War or the evils of fascism. What highly creative artistic activity produces is not a new generalization that transcends established limits, but rather an aesthetic particular. Aesthetic particulars produced by the highly creative artist extend or exploit, in an innovative way, the limits of an existing form, rather than transcend that form.

This is not to deny that a highly creative artist sometimes establishes a new principle of organization in the history of an artistic field; the composer Monteverdi, who created music of the highest aesthetic value, comes to mind. More generally, however, whether or not a composition establishes a new principle in the history of music has little bearing on its aesthetic worth. Because they embody a new principle of organization, some musical works, such as the operas of the Florentine Camerata, are of signal historical importance, but few listeners or musicologists would include these among the great works of music. On the other hand, Mozart's *The Marriage of Figaro* is surely among the masterpieces of music even though its modest innovations are confined to extending existing means. It has been said of Beethoven that he toppled the rules and freed music from the stifling confines of convention. But a close study of his compositions reveals that Beethoven overturned no fundamental rules. Rather, he was an incomparable strategist who exploited limits—the rules, forms, and conventions that he inherited from predecessors such as Haydn and Mozart, Handel and Bach—in strikingly original ways.

21. The author considers a new theory that coherently relates diverse phenomena to one another to be the

(A) basis for reaffirming a well-established scientific formulation
(B) byproduct of an aesthetic experience
(C) tool used by a scientist to discover a new particular
(D) synthesis underlying a great work of art
(E) result of highly creative scientific activity

22. The author implies that Beethoven's music was strikingly original because Beethoven

(A) strove to outdo his predecessors by becoming the first composer to exploit limits
(B) fundamentally changed the musical forms of his predecessors by adopting a richly inventive strategy
(C) embellished and interwove the melodies of several of the great composers who preceded him
(D) manipulated the established conventions of musical composition in a highly innovative fashion
(E) attempted to create the illusion of having transcended the musical forms of his predecessors

23. The passage states that the operas of the Florentine Camerata are

(A) unjustifiably ignored by musicologists
(B) not generally considered to be of high aesthetic value even though they are important in the history of music
(C) among those works in which popular historical themes were portrayed in a musical production
(D) often inappropriately cited as examples of musical works in which a new principle of organization was introduced
(E) minor exceptions to the well-established generalization that the aesthetic worth of a composition determines its importance in the history of music

GO ON TO THE NEXT PAGE.

24. The passage supplies information for answering all of the following questions EXCEPT:

    (A) Has unusual creative activity been characterized as revolutionary?
    (B) Did Beethoven work within a musical tradition that also included Handel and Bach?
    (C) Is Mozart's *The Marriage of Figaro* an example of a creative work that transcended limits?
    (D) Who besides Monteverdi wrote music that the author would consider to embody new principles of organization and to be of high aesthetic value?
    (E) Does anyone claim that the goal of extraordinary creative activity in the arts differs from that of extraordinary creative activity in the sciences?

25. The author regards the idea that all highly creative artistic activity transcends limits with

    (A) deep skepticism
    (B) strong indignation
    (C) marked indifference
    (D) moderate amusement
    (E) sharp derision

26. The author implies that an innovative scientific contribution is one that

    (A) is cited with high frequency in the publications of other scientists
    (B) is accepted immediately by the scientific community
    (C) does not relegate particulars to the role of data
    (D) presents the discovery of a new scientific fact
    (E) introduces a new valid generalization

27. Which of the following statements would most logically conclude the last paragraph of the passage?

    (A) Unlike Beethoven, however, even the greatest of modern composers, such as Stravinsky, did not transcend existing musical forms.
    (B) In similar fashion, existing musical forms were even further exploited by the next generation of great European composers.
    (C) Thus, many of the great composers displayed the same combination of talents exhibited by Monteverdi.
    (D) By contrast, the view that creativity in the arts exploits but does not transcend limits is supported in the field of literature.
    (E) Actually, Beethoven's most original works were largely unappreciated at the time that they were first performed.

GO ON TO THE NEXT PAGE.

Directions: Each question below consists of a word printed in capital letters, followed by five lettered words or phrases. Choose the lettered word or phrase that is most nearly opposite in meaning to the word in capital letters.

Since some of the questions require you to distinguish fine shades of meaning, be sure to consider all the choices before deciding which one is best.

28. BRILLIANCE: (A) dullness   (B) emptiness
    (C) awkwardness   (D) state of immobility
    (E) excess of information

29. QUANDARY:
    (A) state of suppressed enmity
    (B) state of complete certainty
    (C) state of mild hysteria
    (D) state of unprovoked anger
    (E) state of feeble opposition

30. AGGREGATE:
    (A) altered plans
    (B) intended actions
    (C) unexplained occurrences
    (D) isolated units
    (E) unfounded conclusions

31. SUBSTANTIATION: (A) disproof   (B) dissent
    (C) delusion   (D) debate   (E) denial

32. IMPUDENT: (A) compelling   (B) mature
    (C) respectful   (D) thorough   (E) deliberate

33. RECANT: (A) propose   (B) respond
    (C) instruct   (D) affirm   (E) disclose

34. DIVEST: (A) multiply   (B) initiate
    (C) triumph   (D) persist   (E) endow

35. BANALITY:
    (A) accurate portrayal
    (B) impromptu statement
    (C) original expression
    (D) succinct interpretation
    (E) elaborate critique

36. UBIQUITOUS: (A) uniform   (B) unanimous
    (C) unique   (D) anachronistic   (E) mediocre

37. ESCHEW: (A) invest   (B) consume
    (C) maintain   (D) condemn   (E) seek

38. BELIE: (A) flaunt   (B) distend
    (C) attune   (D) obviate   (E) aver

S T O P

IF YOU FINISH BEFORE TIME IS CALLED, YOU MAY CHECK YOUR WORK ON THIS SECTION ONLY.
DO NOT WORK ON ANY OTHER SECTION IN THE TEST.

Section 3 starts on page 38.

SECTION 3
Time—30 minutes
30 Questions

Numbers: All numbers used are real numbers.

Figures: Position of points, angles, regions, etc. can be assumed to be in the order shown; and angle measures can be assumed to be positive.

Lines shown as straight can be assumed to be straight.

Figures can be assumed to lie in a plane unless otherwise indicated.

Figures that accompany questions are intended to provide information useful in answering the questions. However, unless a note states that a figure is drawn to scale, you should solve these problems NOT by estimating sizes by sight or by measurement, but by using your knowledge of mathematics (see Example 2 below).

Directions: Each of the <u>Questions 1-15</u> consists of two quantities, one in Column A and one in Column B. You are to compare the two quantities and choose

      A   if the quantity in Column A is greater;
      B   if the quantity in Column B is greater;
      C   if the two quantities are equal;
      D   if the relationship cannot be determined from the information given.

Note: Since there are only four choices, NEVER MARK (E).

Common Information: In a question, information concerning one or both of the quantities to be compared is centered above the two columns. A symbol that appears in both columns represents the same thing in Column A as it does in Column B.

	Column A	Column B	Sample Answers
Example 1:	2×6	$2 + 6$	● Ⓑ Ⓒ Ⓓ Ⓔ

Examples 2-4 refer to $\triangle PQR$.

	Column A	Column B	Sample Answers
Example 2:	PN	NQ	Ⓐ Ⓑ Ⓒ ● Ⓔ

(since equal measures cannot be assumed, even though PN and NQ appear equal)

	Column A	Column B	Sample Answers
Example 3:	x	y	Ⓐ ● Ⓒ Ⓓ Ⓔ

(since N is between P and Q)

	Column A	Column B	Sample Answers
Example 4:	$w + z$	180	Ⓐ Ⓑ ● Ⓓ Ⓔ

(since PQ is a straight line)

GO ON TO THE NEXT PAGE.

A if the quantity in Column A is greater;
B if the quantity in Column B is greater;
C if the two quantities are equal;
D if the relationship cannot be determined from the information given.

Column A	Column B

1. The value of $(x-5)^2$ when $x=8$ — 6

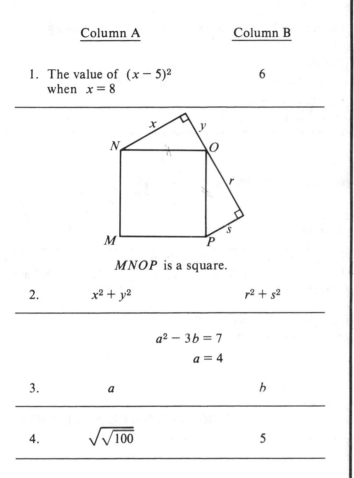

MNOP is a square.

2. $x^2 + y^2$ — $r^2 + s^2$

$$a^2 - 3b = 7$$
$$a = 4$$

3. a — b

4. $\sqrt{\sqrt{100}}$ — 5

Of 65 people polled, 20 percent said that, given the choice among the three colors red, blue, and green, they preferred the color blue.

5. The number of people who said they preferred the color blue — One-half the number of people who said they preferred the color green

Column A	Column B

6. $\dfrac{7 \times 0}{7 + 0}$ — $\dfrac{1}{7}$

$$x > 0 \text{ and } y > 0$$

7. $(2 + x)(3 + y)$ — $6 + xy$

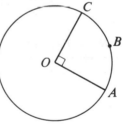

In the correctly worked division problem above, each of the symbols $\square$ and $\triangle$ represents a digit.

8. $\square$ — $\triangle$

O is the center of the circle, and the length of arc *ABC* is 5.

9. The circumference of the circle — 5π

GO ON TO THE NEXT PAGE.

A   if the quantity in Column A is greater;
B   if the quantity in Column B is greater;
C   if the two quantities are equal;
D   if the relationship cannot be determined from the information given.

Column A	Column B

Joanne purchased p pencils and Steve purchased 3 more than half as many pencils as Joanne.

10. The number of $\dfrac{p+6}{2}$
pencils Steve
purchased

---

11. The volume of a can   The volume of a can
that is a right circular   that is a right circular
cylinder with radius   cylinder with radius
of 5 centimeters   of 4 centimeters

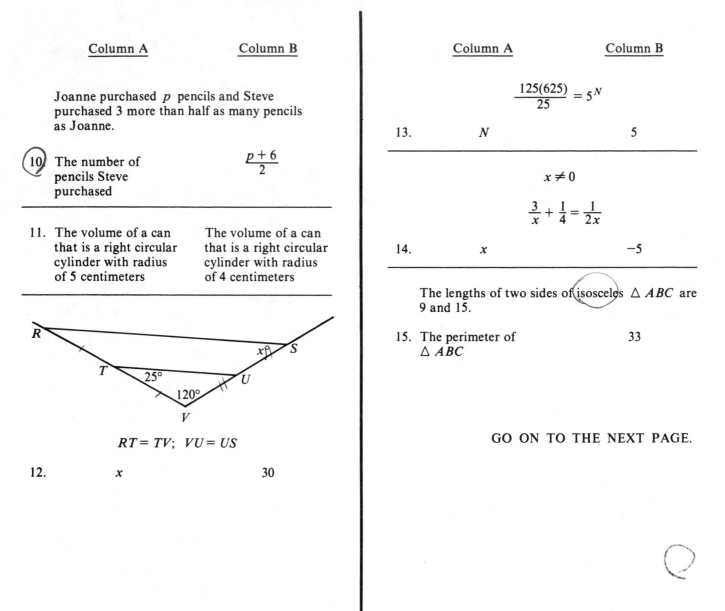

$$RT = TV; \quad VU = US$$

12. x 30

Column A	Column B

$$\frac{125(625)}{25} = 5^N$$

13. N 5

$$x \neq 0$$

$$\frac{3}{x} + \frac{1}{4} = \frac{1}{2x}$$

14. x -5

The lengths of two sides of isosceles $\triangle ABC$ are 9 and 15.

15. The perimeter of   33
$\triangle ABC$

GO ON TO THE NEXT PAGE.

Directions: Each of the Questions 16-30 has five answer choices. For each of these questions, select the best of the answer choices given.

---

16. If $\frac{x}{y} = \frac{3}{4}$, then $\frac{x+y}{y} =$

    (A) $\frac{3}{7}$ (B) $\frac{4}{7}$ (C) 1 (D) $\frac{11}{7}$ (E) $\frac{7}{4}$

17. Which of the following numbers is both a factor of 48 and a multiple of 6 ?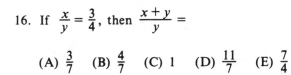

    (A) 2 (B) 8 (C) 12 (D) 16 (E) 18

18. If $2^n = 32$, then $n^2 =$

    (A)   25
    (B)   32
    (C)   64
    (D)   256
    (E) 1,024

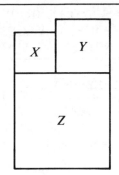

19. The figure above shows how three square flower beds X, Y, and Z are situated. If the area of X is 36 square meters and the area of Y is 64 square meters, what is the area, in square meters, of Z ?

    (A) 100
    (B) 169
    (C) 196
    (D) 200
    (E) 225

20. In a certain room, all except 18 of the people are over 50 years of age. If 15 of the people in the room are under 50 years of age, how many people are in the room?

    (A) 27
    (B) 30
    (C) 33
    (D) 36
    (E) It cannot be determined from the information given.

GO ON TO THE NEXT PAGE.

Questions 21-25 refer to the following chart and information.

LAST WEEK'S TOTAL HOURS WORKED AND HOURLY WAGES FOR THE CASHIERS AT MARKET X

Cashier	Hourly Wage	Total Hours Worked
P	$4.25	40
Q	4.75	32
R	5.00	26
S	5.50	25
T	5.50	22

Note: Last week no more than two cashiers worked at any one time, no cashier worked more than 12 hours on the same day, and on each day each cashier worked continuously.

21. What was the average (arithmetic mean) number of hours that the five cashiers worked last week?

(A) 25
(B) 26
(C) 27
(D) 29
(E) 30

22. What is the least possible number of days on which Cashier R could have worked last week?

(A) 1   (B) 2   (C) 3   (D) 4   (E) 5

23. On Saturday of last week, Market X was open for 15 hours and exactly four cashiers worked. What was the greatest possible amount that the market could have paid in cashiers' wages for that day?

(A) $132.00
(B) $157.50
(C) $161.25
(D) $163.00
(E) $165.00

24. If Market X is open 96 hours per week, for how many hours last week were two cashiers working at the same time?

(A) 49   (B) 48   (C) 36   (D) 24   (E) 12

25. If Cashier S's hourly wage were to increase by 10 percent and S's weekly hours were to decrease by 10 percent from last week's total hours, what would be the change, if any, in S's total weekly wage?

(A) An increase of $1.37
(B) An increase of $0.55
(C) No change
(D) A decrease of $0.55
(E) A decrease of $1.37

GO ON TO THE NEXT PAGE.

26. $|-2| + |7| + |-2+7| =$

    (A) 18
    (B) 14
    (C) 10
    (D) 5
    (E) 0

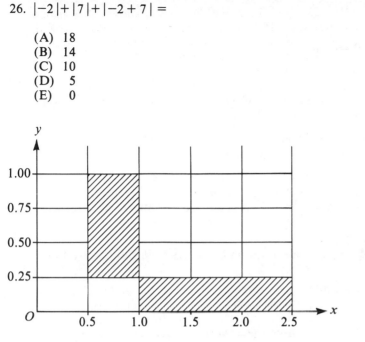

27. What is the sum of the areas of the shaded rectangular regions shown in the figure above?

    (A) 3.0   (B) 2.5   (C) 1.5

    (D) 1.125   (E) 0.75

28. A time-study specialist has set the production rate for each worker on a certain job at 22 units every 3 hours. At this rate what is the minimum number of workers that should be put on the job if at least 90 units are to be produced per hour?

    (A) 5
    (B) 8
    (C) 12
    (D) 13
    (E) 30

29. The volume of the cube in the figure above is 64. If the vertices of $\triangle PQR$ are midpoints of the cube's edges, what is the perimeter of $\triangle PQR$?

    (A) 6
    (B) $6\sqrt{2}$
    (C) $6\sqrt{3}$
    (D) 12
    (E) $12\sqrt{2}$

30. 3×10^4 is greater than 4×10^3 by what percent?

    (A) 25%

    (B) 75%

    (C) $133\frac{1}{3}\%$

    (D) 650%

    (E) 750%

S T O P

IF YOU FINISH BEFORE TIME IS CALLED, YOU MAY CHECK YOUR WORK ON THIS SECTION ONLY.
DO NOT WORK ON ANY OTHER SECTION IN THE TEST.

SECTION 4
Time—30 minutes
30 Questions

Numbers: All numbers used are real numbers.

Figures: Position of points, angles, regions, etc. can be assumed to be in the order shown; and angle measures can be assumed to be positive.

Lines shown as straight can be assumed to be straight.

Figures can be assumed to lie in a plane unless otherwise indicated.

Figures that accompany questions are intended to provide information useful in answering the questions. However, unless a note states that a figure is drawn to scale, you should solve these problems NOT by estimating sizes by sight or by measurement, but by using your knowledge of mathematics (see Example 2 below).

Directions: Each of the <u>Questions 1-15</u> consists of two quantities, one in Column A and one in Column B. You are to compare the two quantities and choose

    A if the quantity in Column A is greater;
    B if the quantity in Column B is greater;
    C if the two quantities are equal;
    D if the relationship cannot be determined from the information given.

Note: Since there are only four choices, **NEVER MARK** (E).

Common
Information: In a question, information concerning one or both of the quantities to be compared is centered above the two columns. A symbol that appears in both columns represents the same thing in Column A as it does in Column B.

Column A	Column B	Sample Answers

Example 1: 2×6 $2 + 6$ ● Ⓑ Ⓒ Ⓓ Ⓔ

Examples 2-4 refer to $\triangle PQR$.

Example 2: PN NQ Ⓐ Ⓑ Ⓒ ● Ⓔ

                           (since equal measures cannot be assumed, even though PN and NQ appear equal)

Example 3: x y Ⓐ ● Ⓒ Ⓓ Ⓔ

                           (since N is between P and Q)

Example 4: $w + z$ 180 Ⓐ Ⓑ ● Ⓓ Ⓔ

                           (since PQ is a straight line)

GO ON TO THE NEXT PAGE.

A if the quantity in Column A is greater;
B if the quantity in Column B is greater;
C if the two quantities are equal;
D if the relationship cannot be determined from the information given.

Column A	Column B

1. $74x + 18$ | 92

2. The number of hours required to travel 1,500 miles at an average speed of 400 miles per hour | The number of hours required to travel 200 miles at an average speed of 50 miles per hour

3. The number of shares of stock X purchased for $1,581,000 | The number of shares of stock Y purchased for $1,603,000

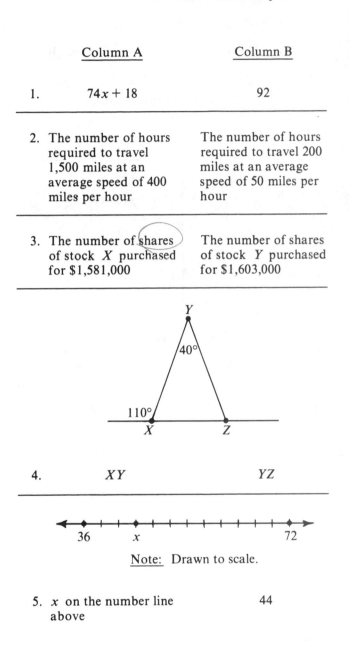

4. XY | YZ

Note: Drawn to scale.

5. x on the number line above | 44

Column A	Column B

$x < 0$

6. $1 - x$ | $x - 1$

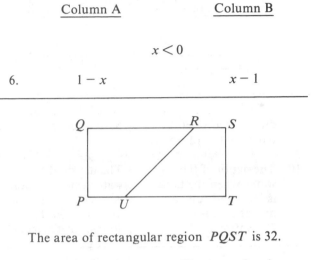

The area of rectangular region $PQST$ is 32.

7. The area of region $PQRU$ | The area of region $RSTU$

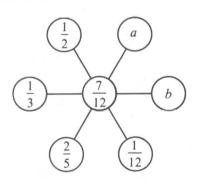

The sum of each pair of numbers in diametrically opposite positions is equal to the number in the center.

8. a | b

GO ON TO THE NEXT PAGE.

A if the quantity in Column A is greater;
B if the quantity in Column B is greater;
C if the two quantities are equal;
D if the relationship cannot be determined from the information given.

Column A	Column B

9. $\dfrac{1}{\frac{1}{3} + \frac{1}{5} + \frac{1}{7}}$ $\qquad$ $\frac{1}{3} + \frac{1}{5} + \frac{1}{7}$

A sealed rectangular tank, which has inside dimensions of 30 by 40 by 50 centimeters, is partially full of water.

10. The depth of the water when the tank is level and rests on one of its 30- by 50-centimeter faces $\qquad$ The depth of the water when the tank is level and rests on one of its 30- by 40-centimeter faces

11. $(4 + \sqrt{5})(4 - \sqrt{5})$ $\qquad$ $(-\sqrt{5} - 4)(\sqrt{5} - 4)$

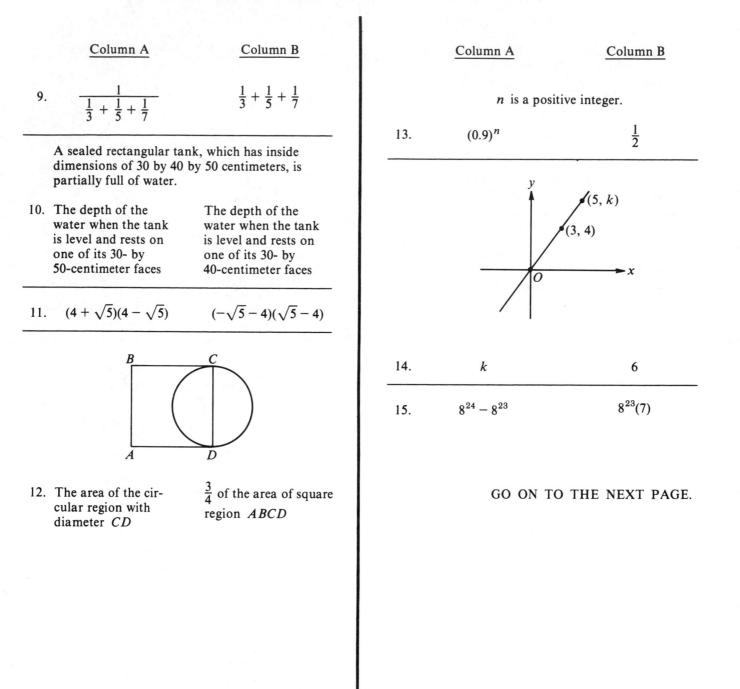

12. The area of the circular region with diameter CD $\qquad$ $\frac{3}{4}$ of the area of square region $ABCD$

Column A	Column B

n is a positive integer.

13. $(0.9)^n$ $\qquad$ $\frac{1}{2}$

14. k $\qquad$ 6

15. $8^{24} - 8^{23}$ $\qquad$ $8^{23}(7)$

GO ON TO THE NEXT PAGE.

Directions: Each of the Questions 16-30 has five answer choices. For each of these questions, select the best of the answer choices given.

16. A linen shop has a certain tablecloth that is available in 8 sizes and 10 colors. What is the maximum possible number of different combinations of size and color available?

(A)   9
(B)   18
(C)   40
(D)   80
(E)   90

17. If $1 - x = 1 + 3x$, then $x =$

(A) 0   (B) $\frac{1}{4}$ (C) $\frac{1}{2}$ (D) $\frac{2}{3}$ (E) 1

18. $\frac{3}{2} + \frac{2}{3} =$

(A) 1   (B) $\frac{7}{6}$ (C) $\frac{4}{3}$ (D) 2   (E) $\frac{13}{6}$

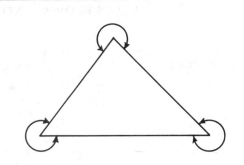

19. In the triangle above, the sum of the measures of the three marked angles is

(A)   540°
(B)   630°
(C)   720°
(D)   810°
(E)   900°

20. Which of the following is greater than 1 ?

(A) $\frac{0.00004}{0.005}$

(B) $\frac{0.000006}{0.0001}$

(C) $\frac{0.01}{0.003}$

(D) $\frac{0.003}{0.006}$

(E) $\frac{0.001}{0.01}$

GO ON TO THE NEXT PAGE.

Questions 21-25 refer to the following graphs.

DOMESTIC AIR CARRIERS: OPERATING REVENUES, MILES FLOWN, AND NUMBER OF PASSENGERS CARRIED, 1960 TO 1975

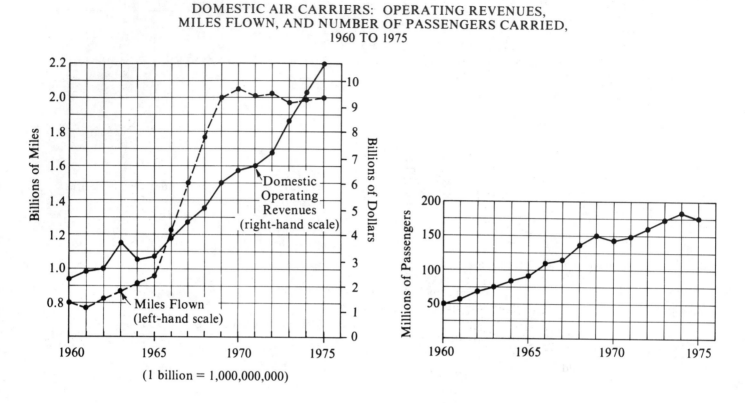

(1 billion = 1,000,000,000)

Note: Graphs drawn to scale.

21. In 1965 how many billions of miles were flown by domestic air carriers?

    (A) 0.95 (B) 1.05 (C) 1.2

    (D) 2.5 (E) 3.0

22. In which of the following years were there more passengers carried by domestic air carriers than in the year before and the year after?

    (A) 1961
    (B) 1965
    (C) 1970
    (D) 1972
    (E) 1974

23. In 1969 what was the ratio of dollars of domestic operating revenues to miles flown?

    (A) $\frac{4}{1}$ (B) $\frac{3}{1}$ (C) $\frac{3}{2}$ (D) $\frac{2}{3}$ (E) $\frac{1}{4}$

24. In billions of miles, approximately what was the average (arithmetic mean) number of miles flown per year by domestic air carriers from 1965 to 1970, inclusive?

    (A) 1.0
    (B) 1.5
    (C) 2.0
    (D) 4.5
    (E) 6.0

25. From 1960 to 1975, what was the percent increase in the number of passengers carried by domestic air carriers?

    (A) 125%
    (B) 175%
    (C) 250%
    (D) 350%
    (E) 450%

GO ON TO THE NEXT PAGE.

26. The average of two numbers is $2x$. If one of the numbers is y, the other number must be

   (A) $x + y$
   (B) $2x + y$
   (C) $4x + y$
   (D) $2x - y$
   (E) $4x - y$

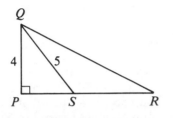

27. In the figure above, the area of triangular region PQR is 36. What is the area of triangular region SQR?

   (A) 30   (B) 24   (C) 18   (D) 15   (E) 12

28. If the ratio of x to y is 9 times the ratio of y to x, then $\frac{x}{y}$ could be

   (A) 9   (B) 3   (C) 1   (D) $\frac{1}{3}$ (E) $\frac{1}{9}$

29. Two microphones are located 100 meters apart and each is 130 meters from the same listening station. If a transmitter is located halfway between the two microphones, what is the distance, in meters, between the transmitter and the listening station?

   (A) 120
   (B) 124
   (C) 125
   (D) 128
   (E) 130

30. A phone call from City X to City Y costs $1.00 for the first 3 minutes and $0.20 for each additional minute. If r is an integer greater than 3, a phone call r minutes long will cost how many <u>dollars</u>?

   (A) $\frac{3r}{5}$

   (B) $\frac{r - 10}{5}$

   (C) $\frac{r - 3}{5}$

   (D) $\frac{r + 2}{5}$

   (E) $\frac{r + 15}{5}$

S T O P

IF YOU FINISH BEFORE TIME IS CALLED, YOU MAY CHECK YOUR WORK ON THIS SECTION ONLY.
DO NOT WORK ON ANY OTHER SECTION IN THE TEST.

SECTION 6

Time—30 minutes

25 Questions

Directions: Each question or group of questions is based on a passage or set of conditions. In answering some of the questions, it may be useful to draw a rough diagram. For each question, select the best answer choice given.

Questions 1-3

Six employees—L, M, N, O, P, and R—are being assigned to offices, each of which can accommodate two persons and no more than two. Each person must be assigned to exactly one office and must be assigned to that office either alone or else together with one other member of the group of six. Enough offices are available to permit any possible assignment of group members to offices, but the following restrictions must be observed:

M cannot share an office with N.
N cannot share an office with O.
P and R must share an office together.

1. Which of the following pairs of employees can be assigned to one office together?

   (A) L and O
   (B) L and R
   (C) N and O
   (D) M and N
   (E) P and M

2. If N is assigned to an office alone, which of the following must be true?

   (A) No one other than N is assigned to an office alone.
   (B) L shares an office with O.
   (C) M is assigned to an office alone.
   (D) The group occupies either 4 or 5 offices.
   (E) The group occupies either 3 or 6 offices.

3. If P and R are the only ones who share an office, how many offices are the minimum that can accommodate the group?

   (A) 2 (B) 3 (C) 4 (D) 5 (E) 6

GO ON TO THE NEXT PAGE.

4. During the month of July in City X, the humidity was always 80 percent or higher whenever the temperature was 75° F or higher. Temperatures that month ranged from 65° to 95° F.

If the statements in the passage above are true, which of the following CANNOT be an accurate report of a temperature and humidity reading for City X in July?

(A) 77° F, 81%
(B) 76° F, 80%
(C) 75° F, 79%
(D) 74° F, 78%
(E) 73° F, 77%

5. Anyone who has owned a car knows that saving money in the short run by skimping on relatively minor repairs and routine maintenance will prove very costly in the long run. However, this basic truth is often forgotten by those who call for reduced government spending on social programs.

Which of the following is NOT implied by the analogy above as a point of comparison?

(A) Money that is spent on repairs and maintenance helps to ensure the continued functioning of a car.
(B) Owners can take chances on not maintaining or repairing their cars.
(C) In order to keep operating, cars will normally need some work.
(D) The problems with a car will become worse if they are not attended to.
(E) A car will last for only a limited period of time and then must be replaced.

6. If athletes want better performances, they should train at high altitudes. At higher altitudes, the body has more red blood cells per unit volume of blood than at sea level. The red blood cells transport oxygen, which will improve performance if available in greater amounts. The blood of an athlete who trains at high altitudes will transport more oxygen per unit volume of blood, improving the athlete's performance.

Which of the following, if true, would be most damaging to the argument above, provided that the athlete's heart rate is the same at high and low altitudes?

(A) Scientists have found that an athlete's heart requires a period of time to adjust to working at high altitudes.
(B) Scientists have found that the body's total volume of blood declines by as much as 25 percent at high altitudes.
(C) Middle-distance runners who train at high altitudes sometimes lose races to middle-distance runners who train at sea level.
(D) The performances of athletes in competitions at all altitudes have improved markedly during the past twenty years.
(E) At altitudes above 5,500 feet, middle-distance runners often better their sea-level running times by several seconds.

GO ON TO THE NEXT PAGE.

<u>Questions 7-13</u>

When they hold a meeting, seven company executives—
T, U, V, W, X, Y, and Z—sit at a rectangular table.
Three executives sit along one side of the table, and three
sit along the other side, each directly opposite one of the
other three. The seventh sits at the head of the table;
there is no seat at the foot of the table.

    U always sits in one of the two seats farthest from
      the head of the table.

    Y and V always sit next to each other.

    V never sits next to Z.

    If Z does not sit at the head of the table, W sits
      there.

7. Which of the following is an acceptable seating
    arrangement of the executives, starting with U,
    moving toward the head of the table, and con-
    tinuing around the table?

    (A) U, X, T, Z, V, Y, W
    (B) U, T, X, Z, Y, V, W
    (C) U, X, Z, Y, V, W, T
    (D) U, Z, W, X, V, Y, T
    (E) U, T, X, W, Z, V, Y

8. If W sits directly opposite T, X must sit next to
    which of the following executives?

    (A) T   (B) U   (C) V   (D) Y   (E) Z

9. If T sits directly opposite Z and next to V, which
    executive must sit directly opposite U ?

    (A) V   (B) W   (C) X   (D) Y   (E) Z

10. If Z sits directly opposite X, which executive must
    sit next to U ?

    (A) T   (B) V   (C) W   (D) Y   (E) Z

11. If T and U sit immediately on either side of X, the
    executive sitting directly opposite X must be either

    (A) W or V   (B) W or Z   (C) Y or V
    (D) Y or Z   (E) Z or V

12. If W sits directly opposite U and next to T, the
    two executives sitting immediately on either side
    of X must be

    (A) Y and V   (B) Y and W   (C) T and Z
    (D) T and V   (E) Z and W

13. If Z sits at the head of the table, Y directly
    opposite U, and V immediately on X's left, what
    is the total number of possible seating arrange-
    ments of the executives?

    (A) 1   (B) 2   (C) 3   (D) 4   (E) 5

GO ON TO THE NEXT PAGE.

Questions 14-16

A weaver who is working on six rugs—G, H, I, J, K, and L—is preparing a work schedule for a work week consisting of five consecutive workdays— Monday through Friday. Rugs G, H, and I are of pattern 1, rugs J and K are of pattern 2, and rug L is of pattern 3. The work must be scheduled in accordance with the following conditions:

The weaver must work on each of the six rugs during the work week.

The weaver cannot work on the same rug on two consecutive days.

On any day that the weaver works on rug G, the weaver must work on rug J; the weaver cannot work on rug L that day.

On any day that the weaver works on more than one rug, those rugs must all be of different patterns.

14. The weaver could schedule work on which of the following rugs for the same day?

(A) G, J, and L
(B) G, I, and K
(C) G, J, and K
(D) H, I, and L
(E) H, J, and L

15. If the weaver's decision is to work on rug J on Tuesday, the weaver CANNOT work on rug

(A) G on Monday
(B) H on Tuesday
(C) I on Wednesday
(D) K on Thursday
(E) L on Friday

16. If the weaver's decision is to work on rug G on Monday and Friday only, and on rug K on Wednesday only, the weaver must work on a rug of pattern 2 on exactly how many workdays?

(A) 1　(B) 2　(C) 3　(D) 4　(E) 5

GO ON TO THE NEXT PAGE.

53

Questions 17-22

Ruth, Sandra, Thea, and Ulla are the four finalists in a contest in which they perform set exercises on a balance beam. In each round of the contest, different exercises must be attempted. A contestant is eliminated the first time she fails at any of the exercises. To reduce any effect that the relative order of contestants within rounds may have on their performance, their relative order must be changed in going from one round to the next if it is possible to do so by executing one of the following three alternative reorderings between rounds:

X: Move the previously third contestant directly in front of the previously second contestant.
Y: Move the previously third contestant directly in front of the previously first contestant.
Z: Move the previously last contestant into first position.

If a contestant mentioned in a reordering has just been eliminated, that reordering cannot be executed.

If none of the reorderings can be executed, the remaining contestants must perform in the same order relative to each other as in the previous round.

17. If the order of contestants in one round is Ulla, Ruth, Sandra, Thea, and if Sandra is alone in being eliminated in that round, the order of contestants for the next round must be which of the following?

(A) Ruth, Thea, Ulla
(B) Ruth, Ulla, Thea
(C) Thea, Ruth, Ulla
(D) Thea, Ulla, Ruth
(E) Ulla, Ruth, Thea

18. If the order of contestants in one round is Sandra, Ruth, Thea, Ulla, and if none of the contestants is eliminated in that round, it must be true that in the next round

(A) Ruth is third
(B) Sandra is second
(C) Thea is first
(D) Ulla is first
(E) Ulla is fourth

19. The elimination of which of the following pairs of contestants in a round in which all four contestants competed would have the consequence that the relative position of the remaining contestants remains unchanged?

(A) Those competing first and second
(B) Those competing first and third
(C) Those competing second and third
(D) Those competing second and fourth
(E) Those competing third and fourth

20. If the order of contestants in a round in which no one fails is Ruth, Thea, Ulla, Sandra, the order of contestants in the next round could be which of the following?

(A) Ruth, Sandra, Ulla, Thea
(B) Sandra, Ruth, Ulla, Thea
(C) Sandra, Ulla, Ruth, Thea
(D) Thea, Ruth, Ulla, Sandra
(E) Ulla, Ruth, Thea, Sandra

21. If none of the four contestants is eliminated in the course of the first two rounds, and if the order of contestants in the third round is the same as it was in the first round, which of the following must have been the two reorderings executed so far?

(A) X, twice
(B) Z, twice
(C) X, followed by Y
(D) Y, followed by X
(E) Z, followed by Y

22. If the order of contestants in one round is Thea, Sandra, Ulla, Ruth, and if Sandra remains in second position afterward, which of the following could have happened?

(A) None of the contestants was eliminated in the round, and X was executed.
(B) Ruth alone was eliminated in the round, and X was executed.
(C) Thea alone was eliminated in the round, and Y was executed.
(D) Ulla alone was eliminated in the round, and Z was executed.
(E) Thea alone was eliminated in the round, and Z was executed.

GO ON TO THE NEXT PAGE.

23. M is heavier than Q, but it is lighter than R.
    S is heavier than Q and it is also heavier than R.
    U is heavier than Q and it is also heavier than R.

    If the statements above are true, one can conclude
    with certainty that T is heavier than M if one
    knows in addition that

    (A) S weighs the same as U weighs
    (B) S is heavier than T
    (C) T is heavier than Q
    (D) T is heavier than U
    (E) U is heavier than M

24. The cost of the average computer logic device is
    falling at the rate of 25 percent per year, and the
    cost of the average computer memory device at the
    rate of 40 percent per year. It can be concluded that
    if these rates of cost decline remain constant for a
    period of three years, at the end of that time the cost
    of the average computer memory device will have
    declined by a greater amount than the cost of the
    average computer logic device.

    Accurate information about which of the following
    would be most useful in evaluating the correctness
    of the conclusion above?

    (A) The number of logic devices and memory
        devices projected to be purchased during the
        next three years
    (B) The actual prices charged for the average com-
        puter logic device and the average computer
        memory device
    (C) The compatibility of different manufacturers'
        logic devices and memory devices
    (D) The relative durability of logic devices and
        memory devices
    (E) The average number of logic devices and mem-
        ory devices needed for an average computer
        system

25. Earthquakes, volcanic eruptions, and unusual
    weather have caused many more natural disasters
    adversely affecting people in the past decade than
    in previous decades. We can conclude that the
    planet Earth as a natural environment has become
    more inhospitable and dangerous, and we should
    employ the weather and earth sciences to look for
    causes of this trend.

    The conclusion drawn above is most seriously
    weakened if which of the following is true?

    (A) The weather and earth sciences have provided
        better early warning systems for natural
        disasters in the past decade than in previous
        decades.
    (B) International relief efforts for victims of
        natural disasters have been better organized
        in the past decade than in previous decades.
    (C) There are records of major earthquakes,
        volcanic eruptions, droughts, landslides, and
        floods occurring in the distant past, as well
        as in the recent past.
    (D) Population pressures and poverty have forced
        increasing numbers of people to live in areas
        prone to natural disasters.
    (E) There have been no changes in the past decade
        in people's land-use practices that could
        have affected the climate.

S T O P

IF YOU FINISH BEFORE TIME IS CALLED, YOU MAY CHECK YOUR WORK ON THIS SECTION ONLY.
DO NOT WORK ON ANY OTHER SECTION IN THE TEST.

SECTION 7

Time—30 minutes

25 Questions

Directions: Each question or group of questions is based on a passage or set of conditions. In answering some of the questions, it may be useful to draw a rough diagram. For each question, select the best answer choice given.

Questions 1-5

Because of a computer malfunction, an accountant cannot directly determine the classification of certain accounts. Each account falls into one of five classifications: type 1, type 2, type 3, type 4, or type 5. The accountant hopes to be able to determine the classification of these accounts by tracing which operations the computer has performed on them. There are exactly four operations: W, X, Y, and Z. No operation can be performed more than once on a given account, and the operations were performed, without exception, according to the following rules:

If an account is a type 1, the computer performs either operation W or, alternatively, operation X.

If the account is a type 2, the computer performs either operation X alone or, alternatively, operation X and any one of the remaining operations except W.

If an account is a type 3, the computer performs either operation Y alone or, alternatively, operation Y and any one of the remaining operations.

If an account is a type 4, the computer performs exactly two operations in any combination except that X cannot be one of the two operations.

If an account is a type 5, the computer performs exactly three operations in any combination drawn from the four operations.

1. If the accountant knows that the computer has performed exactly one operation on an account, which of the following must be true?

(A) The account is either a type 1 or a type 2.
(B) The account is either a type 1, a type 2, or a type 3.
(C) The account is either a type 2, a type 3, or a type 5.
(D) The account is either a type 2, a type 4, or a type 5.
(E) The account is either a type 3, a type 4, or a type 5.

2. If the accountant knows that the computer has performed operation Z on an account but cannot determine solely from traces in the account whether any other operation has been performed, the account could be any one of the five types EXCEPT type

(A) 1
(B) 2
(C) 3
(D) 4
(E) 5

3. Which type of account, if operated on by the computer, must have operation X performed on it?

(A) Type 1
(B) Type 2
(C) Type 3
(D) Type 4
(E) Type 5

4. If the accountant knows that operations X and Z are the only operations that have been performed on an account, the account must be a type

(A) 1
(B) 2
(C) 3
(D) 4
(E) 5

5. If the accountant knows that the computer has performed exactly two operations on a given account, and operation Y was not one of the two, which of the following must be true?

(A) The account is either a type 1 or a type 2.
(B) The account is either a type 2 or a type 3.
(C) The account is either a type 2 or a type 4.
(D) The account is either a type 3 or a type 4.
(E) The account is either a type 3 or a type 5.

GO ON TO THE NEXT PAGE.

6. At the end of the Second World War the number of women in their childbearing years was at a record low. Yet for almost twenty years they produced a record high number of children. In 1957 there was an average of 3.72 children per family. Now the postwar babies are producing a record low number of babies. In 1983 the average number of children per family was about 1.79—two children fewer than the 1957 rate and lower even than the 2.11 rate that a population needs to replace itself.

It can properly be inferred from the passage that

(A) for the birth rate to be high, there must be a relatively large number of women in their childbearing years
(B) the most significant factor influencing the birth rate is whether the country is engaged in a war
(C) unless there are extraordinary circumstances, the birth rate will not dip below the level at which a population replaces itself
(D) for the birth rate to be low, there must be a relatively small number of women in their childbearing years
(E) the birth rate is not directly proportional to the number of women in their childbearing years

7. A study of illusionistic painting incvitably begins with the Greek painter Zeuxis. In an early work, which is the basis for his fame, he painted a bowl of grapes that was so lifelike that birds pecked at the fruit. In an attempt to expand his achievement to encompass human figures, he painted a boy carrying a bunch of grapes. When birds immediately came to peck at the fruit, Zeuxis judged that he had failed.

Zeuxis' judgment that he had failed in his later work was based on an assumption. Which of the following can have served as that assumption?

(A) People are more easily fooled by illusionistic techniques than are birds.
(B) The use of illusionistic techniques in painting had become commonplace by the time Zeuxis completed his later work.
(C) The grapes in the later painting were even more realistic than the ones in the earlier work.
(D) Birds are less likely to peck at fruit when they see that a human being is present.
(E) After the success of his early work, Zeuxis was unable to live up to the expectations of the general public.

8. The best argument for the tenure system that protects professional employment in universities is that it allows veteran faculty to hire people smarter than they are and yet remain secure in the knowledge that unless they themselves are caught in an act of moral turpitude—a concept that in the present climate almost defies definition—the younger faculty cannot turn around and fire them. This is not true in industry.

Which of the following assumptions is most likely to have been made by the author of the argument above?

(A) Industry should follow the example of universities and protect the jobs of managers by instituting a tenure system.
(B) If no tenure system existed, veteran faculty would be reluctant to hire new faculty who might threaten the veteran faculty's own jobs.
(C) The traditional argument that the tenure system protects scholars in universities from being dismissed for holding unconventional or unpopular beliefs is no longer persuasive.
(D) If a stronger consensus concerning what constitutes moral turpitude existed, the tenure system in universities would be expendable.
(E) Veteran faculty will usually hire and promote new faculty whose scholarship is more up-to-date than their own.

GO ON TO THE NEXT PAGE.

Questions 9-15

The appellate court of a state in the United States is staffed by exactly eight judges—R, S, T, U, V, W, X, and Y. At the beginning of each session of the court, the clerk of the court announces two panels of three judges each, one to hear criminal cases and one to hear civil cases.

> No judge can serve on more than one panel at a session of the court.
>
> At least two members of the panel hearing criminal cases must have had prior experience with criminal cases. The judges with experience in criminal cases, listed in order of descending seniority, are R, S, T, and U.
>
> At least two members of the panel hearing civil cases must have had prior experience with civil cases. The judges with experience in civil cases, listed in order of descending seniority, are V, W, X, and Y.
>
> The presiding judge of each panel is the judge among the three on the panel with the greatest seniority in the area of the cases.
>
> Each of the three major geographical regions of the state must be represented on every panel by exactly one judge. Judges S and W are from the western part of the state; Judges R, U, and Y are from the central part of the state; and Judges T, V, and X are from the eastern part of the state.
>
> If a judge cannot serve on a panel because of illness or conflict of interest, his or her place can be taken only by a judge who meets the necessary conditions for the panel.

9. Which of the following could be the panel of judges selected to hear civil cases?

(A) R, S, V
(B) S, U, X
(C) T, W, Y
(D) U, V, Y
(E) V, X, Y

10. If X is the presiding judge of the panel selected to hear civil cases, which of the following must be the other two members of that panel?

(A) R and W
(B) S and U
(C) S and Y
(D) T and Y
(E) U and V

11. Which of the following could be the panel of judges selected to hear criminal cases?

(A) R, S, X
(B) R, V, W
(C) S, T, W
(D) S, V, Y
(E) T, U, X

12. The judges selected to serve on any panel announced by the clerk of the court must include either

(A) R or U
(B) R or Y
(C) S or W
(D) T or V
(E) T or X

13. If the panel of judges hearing criminal cases consists of T, U, and W, and if U withdraws because of a conflict of interest and is replaced, which of the following judges will be the presiding judge of the panel hearing criminal cases after U has been replaced?

(A) R   (B) S   (C) T   (D) W   (E) Y

14. If V cannot serve on either panel and if the panel of judges hearing civil cases consists of U, W, and X, all of the following must be true EXCEPT:

(A) S is a member of the panel hearing criminal cases.
(B) T is a member of the panel hearing criminal cases.
(C) T is the presiding judge of the panel hearing criminal cases.
(D) W is the presiding judge of the panel hearing civil cases.
(E) Either R or Y, but not both, is a member of the panel hearing criminal cases.

15. If the panel of judges hearing criminal cases consists of T, U, and W, and if X is appointed as a replacement on the panel hearing civil cases, after that change which of the following judges will be the presiding judge of the panel hearing civil cases?

(A) S   (B) V   (C) W   (D) X   (E) Y

GO ON TO THE NEXT PAGE.

Questions 16-19

A cryptanalyst must translate into letters all of the digits included in the following two lines of nine symbols each:

9 3 3 4 5 6 6 6 7
2 2 3 3 4 4 5 7 8

The cryptanalyst has already determined some of the rules governing the decoding:

Each of the digits from 2 to 9 represents exactly one of the eight letters A, E, I, O, U, R, S, and T, and each letter is represented by exactly one of the digits.
If a digit occurs more than once, it represents the same letter on each occasion.
The letter T and the letter O are each represented exactly 3 times.
The letter I and the letter A are each represented exactly two times.
The letter E is represented exactly four times.

16. If 2 represents R and 7 represents A, then 5 must represent

   (A) I   (B) O   (C) S   (D) T   (E) U

17. Which of the following is a possible decoding of the five-digit message 4 6 5 3 6 ?

   (A) O–T–A–E–T
   (B) O–T–E–U–T
   (C) O–O–S–E–O
   (D) T–O–I–E–T
   (E) T–O–R–E–T

18. If 9 represents a vowel, it must represent which of the following?

   (A) A   (B) E   (C) I   (D) O   (E) U

19. If 8 represents a vowel, which of the following must represent a consonant?

   (A) 2   (B) 4   (C) 5   (D) 7   (E) 9

GO ON TO THE NEXT PAGE.

Questions 20-22

An instructor regularly offers a six-week survey course on film genres. Each time the course is given, she covers six of the following eight genres: adventure films, *cinéma noir*, detective films, fantasy films, horror films, musical comedies, silent films, and westerns. She will discuss exactly one genre per week according to the following conditions:

Silent films are always covered, and always in the first week.

Westerns and adventure films are always covered, with westerns covered in the week immediately preceding the week adventure films are covered.

Musical comedies are never covered in the same course in which fantasy films are covered.

If detective films are covered, they are covered after westerns are covered, with exactly one of the other genres covered between them.

Cinéma noir is not covered unless detective films are covered in one of the previous weeks.

20. Which of the following is an acceptable schedule of genres for weeks one through six of the course?

(A) Silent films, westerns, adventure films, detective films, horror films, musical comedies
(B) Silent films, westerns, adventure films, horror films, detective films, fantasy films
(C) Fantasy films, musical comedies, detective films, *cinéma noir*, westerns, adventure films
(D) Westerns, adventure films, detective films, *cinéma noir*, musical comedies, horror films
(E) Detective films, westerns, adventure films, horror films, fantasy films, *cinéma noir*

21. If musical comedies are covered the week immediately preceding the week westerns are covered, which of the following can be true?

(A) Adventure films are covered the second week.
(B) *Cinéma noir* is covered the fourth week.
(C) Detective films are covered the third week.
(D) Fantasy films are covered the fifth week.
(E) Horror films are covered the sixth week.

22. Which of the following will NEVER be covered in the sixth week of the course?

(A) *Cinéma noir* (B) Fantasy films
(C) Horror films (D) Musical comedies
(E) Westerns

23. The population of elephant seals, reduced by hunting to perhaps a few dozen animals early in this century, has soared under federal protection during the last few decades. However, because the species repopulated itself through extensive inbreeding, it now exhibits a genetic uniformity that is almost unparalleled in other species of mammals, and thus it is in far greater danger of becoming extinct than are most other species.

Given the information in the passage above, which of the following is most likely the reason that other species of mammals are less likely than elephant seals to become extinct?

(A) Other species of mammals have large populations, so the loss of a few members of the species is not significant.
(B) Other species of mammals have increased their knowledge of dangers through the experience of generation after generation of animals.
(C) In other species of mammals, hunters can readily distinguish between males and females or between young animals and adults.
(D) In other species of mammals, some members of the species are genetically better equipped to withstand a disease or event that destroys other members of the species.
(E) Other species of mammals have retained habits of caution and alertness because they have not been protected as endangered species.

GO ON TO THE NEXT PAGE.

24. Some people assert that prosecutors should be allowed to introduce illegally obtained evidence in criminal trials if the judge and jury can be persuaded that the arresting officer was not aware of violating or did not intend to violate the law while seizing the evidence. This proposed "good-faith exception" would weaken everyone's constitutional protection, lead to less careful police practices, and promote lying by law enforcement officers in court.

The argument above for maintaining the prohibition against illegally obtained evidence assumes that

(A) defendants in criminal cases should enjoy greater protection from the law than other citizens do

(B) law enforcement authorities need to be encouraged to pursue criminals assiduously

(C) the legal system will usually find ways to ensure that real crimes do not go unprosecuted

(D) the prohibition now deters some unlawful searches and seizures

(E) courts should consider the motives of law enforcement officers in deciding whether evidence brought forward by the officers is admissible in a trial

25. If it is true that the streets and the sidewalks are wet whenever it is raining, which of the following must also be true?

   I. If the streets and sidewalks are wet, it is raining.
   II. If the streets are wet but the sidewalks are not wet, it is not raining.
   III. If it is not raining, the streets and sidewalks are not wet.

(A) I only
(B) II only
(C) III only
(D) I and II only
(E) II and III only

S T O P

IF YOU FINISH BEFORE TIME IS CALLED, YOU MAY CHECK YOUR WORK ON THIS SECTION ONLY.
DO NOT WORK ON ANY OTHER SECTION IN THE TEST.

THE GRADUATE RECORD EXAMINATIONS
GENERAL TEST

You will have 3 hours and 30 minutes in which to work on this test, which consists of seven sections. During the time allowed for one section, you may work only on that section. The time allowed for each section is 30 minutes.

Your score will be based on the number of questions for which you select the best answer choice given. No deduction will be made for a question for which you do not select the best answer choice given. Therefore, you are advised to answer all questions.

You are advised to work as rapidly as you can without losing accuracy. Do not spend too much time on questions that are too difficult for you. Go on to the other questions and come back to the difficult ones later.

There are several different types of questions; you will find special directions for each type in the test itself. Be sure you understand the directions before attempting to answer any questions.

For each question several answer choices (lettered A-E or A-D) are given from which you are to select the ONE best answer. YOU MUST INDICATE ALL OF YOUR ANSWERS ON THE SEPARATE ANSWER SHEET. No credit will be given for anything written in this examination book, but to work out your answers you may write in the book as much as you wish. After you have decided which of the suggested answers is best, blacken the corresponding space on the answer sheet. Be sure to:

- Use a soft black lead pencil (No. 2 or HB).

- Mark only one answer to each question. No credit will be given for multiple answers.

- Mark your answer in the row with the same number as the number of the question you are answering.

- Carefully and completely blacken the space corresponding to the answer you select for each question. Fill the space with a dark mark so that you cannot see the letter inside the space. Light or partial marks may not be read by the scoring machine. See the example of proper and improper answer marks below.

- Erase all stray marks. If you change an answer, be sure that you completely erase the old answer before marking your new answer. Incomplete erasures may be read as intended answers.

Example:

Sample Answer

What city is the capital of France?

  Ⓐ ● Ⓒ Ⓓ Ⓔ   BEST ANSWER PROPERLY MARKED

(A) Rome

(B) Paris

(C) London

(D) Cairo

(E) Oslo

  Ⓐ Ⓧ Ⓒ Ⓓ Ⓔ

  Ⓐ Ⓑ Ⓒ Ⓓ Ⓔ   IMPROPER MARKS

  Ⓐ Ⓑ Ⓒ Ⓓ Ⓔ

  Ⓐ Ⓑ Ⓒ Ⓓ Ⓔ

Do not be concerned that the answer sheet provides spaces for more answers than there are questions in the test. Some or all of the passages for this test have been adapted from published material to provide the examinee with significant problems for analysis and evaluation. To make the passages suitable for testing purposes, the style, content, or point of view of the original may have been altered in some cases. The ideas contained in the passages do not necessarily represent the opinions of the Graduate Record Examinations Board or Educational Testing Service.

CLOSE YOUR TEST BOOK AND WAIT FOR FURTHER INSTRUCTIONS FROM THE SUPERVISOR.

I

NOTE: To ensure the prompt and accurate processing of test results, your cooperation in following these directions is needed. The procedures that follow have been kept to the minimum necessary. They will take a few minutes to complete, but it is essential that you fill in all blanks <u>exactly</u> as directed.

GENERAL TEST

A. Print and sign your full name in this box:

| PRINT: _____ |
| (LAST)　　　　　　　(FIRST)　　　　　　　(MIDDLE) |
| SIGN: _____ |

B. Your answer sheet contains areas which will be used to ensure accurate reporting of your test results. It is essential that you fill in these areas <u>exactly</u> as explained below.

1. YOUR NAME, MAILING ADDRESS, AND TEST CENTER: Place your answer sheet so that the heading "Graduate Record Examinations—General Test" is at the top. In box 1 below that heading <u>print</u> your name. Enter your current mailing address. Print the name of the city, state or province, and country in which the test center is located, and the center number.

2. YOUR NAME: <u>Print</u> all the information requested in the boxes at the top of the columns (first four letters of your last name, your first initial, and middle initial), and then fill in completely the appropriate space beneath each entry.

3. DATE OF BIRTH: Fill in completely the space beside the month in which you were born. Then enter the day of the month on which you were born in the boxes at the top of the columns. Fill in completely the appropriate space beneath each entry. Be sure to treat zeros like any other digit, and to add a zero before any single digit; for example 03, not 3. (Your year of birth is not required on the answer sheet.)

4. SEX: Fill in completely the appropriate space.

5. REGISTRATION NUMBER: Copy your registration number from your admission ticket into the boxes at the top of the columns and then fill in completely the appropriate space beneath each entry. Check your admission ticket again to make certain that you have copied your registration number accurately.

6. TITLE CODE: Copy the numbers shown below and fill in completely the appropriate spaces beneath each entry as shown. When you have completed item 6, check to be sure it is identical to the illustration below.

| 6. TITLE CODE |
| 0 | 4 | 0 | 1 | 4 |

7. CERTIFICATION STATEMENT: In the boxed area, please write (do not print) the following statement: I certify that I am the person whose name appears on this answer sheet. I also agree not to disclose the contents of the test I am taking today to anyone. Sign and date where indicated.

8. FORM CODE: Copy **GR 87-4** in the box.

9. TEST BOOK SERIAL NUMBER: Copy the serial number of your test book in the box. It is printed in red at the upper right on the front cover of your test book.

C. WHEN YOU HAVE FINISHED THESE INSTRUCTIONS, PLEASE TURN YOUR ANSWER SHEET OVER AND SIGN YOUR NAME IN THE BOX EXACTLY AS YOU DID FOR ITEM 7.

When you have finished, wait for further instructions from the supervisor. DO NOT OPEN YOUR TEST BOOK UNTIL YOU ARE TOLD TO DO SO.

FOR GENERAL TEST, FORM GR87-4 ONLY
Answer Key and Percentages* of Examinees Answering Each Question Correctly

VERBAL ABILITY						QUANTITATIVE ABILITY						ANALYTICAL ABILITY					
Section 1			Section 2			Section 3			Section 4			Section 6			Section 7		
Number	Answer	P+	Number	Answer	P+	Number	Answer	P+	Number	Answer	P+	Number	Answer	P+	Number	Answer	P+
1	C	90	1	E	91	1	A	95	1	D	83	1	A	94	1	B	74
2	D	85	2	E	91	2	C	87	2	B	86	2	D	76	2	A	79
3	B	63	3	D	89	3	A	89	3	D	93	3	D	68	3	B	86
4	E	58	4	E	66	4	B	90	4	C	83	4	C	90	4	B	82
5	D	49	5	D	57	5	D	85	5	A	80	5	E	72	5	C	60
6	A	45	6	C	53	6	B	92	6	A	82	6	B	72	6	E	84
7	B	25	7	C	26	7	A	71	7	D	76	7	B	76	7	D	75
8	B	83	8	C	91	8	B	76	8	B	73	8	B	58	8	B	69
9	C	82	9	E	85	9	A	64	9	A	62	9	D	60	9	C	61
10	D	67	10	C	75	10	C	63	10	B	66	10	A	68	10	C	59
11	E	56	11	A	55	11	D	57	11	C	54	11	C	68	11	A	76
12	D	52	12	B	47	12	A	65	12	A	47	12	C	65	12	C	59
13	B	46	13	B	59	13	C	49	13	D	52	13	B	56	13	A	61
14	B	34	14	E	50	14	B	41	14	A	33	14	E	55	14	C	50
15	A	33	15	A	24	15	D	49	15	C	23	15	A	57	15	D	31
16	E	19	16	A	22	16	E	88	16	D	93	16	C	54	16	A	66
17	D	82	17	B	83	17	C	79	17	A	87	17	D	48	17	A	49
18	B	67	18	A	33	18	A	82	18	E	89	18	A	34	18	E	67
19	E	82	19	E	81	19	C	77	19	E	63	19	E	34	19	E	40
20	E	41	20	A	55	20	E	73	20	C	79	20	E	42	20	A	54
21	C	78	21	E	48	21	D	86	21	A	87	21	A	32	21	E	37
22	A	63	22	D	53	22	C	81	22	E	76	22	E	20	22	E	50
23	D	73	23	B	74	23	C	48	23	B	52	23	D	49	23	D	57
24	A	29	24	D	45	24	A	29	24	B	73	24	B	55	24	D	43
25	E	40	25	A	36	25	E	37	25	C	43	25	D	33	25	B	43
26	D	52	26	E	46	26	B	64	26	E	52						
27	B	50	27	B	49	27	E	54	27	A	42						
28	D	87	28	A	91	28	D	51	28	B	36						
29	C	85	29	B	78	29	B	40	29	A	48						
30	E	77	30	D	73	30	D	18	30	D	37						
31	D	70	31	A	75												
32	D	54	32	C	67												
33	E	58	33	D	53												
34	A	44	34	E	47												
35	D	32	35	C	45												
36	E	43	36	C	37												
37	A	25	37	E	18												
38	C	17	38	E	16												

*Estimated P+ for the group of examinees who took the GRE General Test in a recent three-year period.

SCORE CONVERSIONS AND PERCENTS BELOW* for GRE GENERAL TEST, FORM GR87-4 ONLY

Raw Score	Verbal Score	% Below	Quantitative Score	% Below	Analytical Score	% Below	Raw Score	Verbal Score	% Below	Quantitative Score	% Below	Analytical Score	% Below
74-76	800	99					40	440	40	560	52	650	84
73	790	99					39	430	37	540	46	640	81
72	780	99					38	420	34	530	44	630	78
71	770	99					37	410	31	520	42	620	77
							36	410	31	510	39	600	72
70	760	99											
69	740	98					35	400	28	500	37	590	69
68	730	97					34	390	26	480	32	580	67
67	720	96					33	380	24	470	30	570	64
66	710	96					32	370	22	460	27	560	61
							31	360	18	450	26	540	56
65	700	95											
64	680	93					30	360	18	430	21	530	53
63	670	92					29	350	17	420	19	520	50
62	660	91					28	340	15	410	18	510	46
61	650	89					27	330	13	400	16	490	41
							26	330	13	390	14	480	38
60	640	88	800	98									
59	630	86	790	98			25	320	11	370	11	470	36
58	620	85	780	97			24	310	10	360	10	450	30
57	610	84	760	94			23	300	8	350	9	440	27
56	590	80	750	92			22	290	7	340	8	430	25
							21	280	6	320	6	410	21
55	580	78	740	90									
54	570	75	730	89			20	270	4	310	5	400	18
53	560	73	720	87			19	260	3	300	4	390	16
52	550	71	700	83			18	250	3	290	3	380	15
51	540	68	690	81			17	240	2	280	3	360	11
							16	230	1	260	2	350	10
50	530	65	680	79	800	99							
49	520	63	670	77	800	99	15	220	1	250	1	330	7
48	510	60	650	72	780	98	14	210	1	240	1	310	5
47	510	60	640	71	760	97	13	200	0	230	1	300	4
46	500	57	630	68	740	95	12	200	0	210	0	280	3
							11	200	0	200	0	260	2
45	480	52	620	65	720	93							
44	470	49	610	63	710	92	10	200	0	200	0	240	1
43	470	49	590	59	690	89	9	200	0	200	0	230	1
42	460	45	580	56	680	88	8	200	0	200	0	210	0
41	450	43	570	53	670	86	0-7	200	0	200	0	200	0

*Percent scoring below the scaled score, based on the performance of the 816,621 examinees who took the General Test between October 1, 1983, and September 30, 1986.

FORM GR 87-5

01

THE GRADUATE RECORD
EXAMINATIONS

General Test

SECTION 1

Time—30 minutes

38 Questions

Directions: Each sentence below has one or two blanks, each blank indicating that something has been omitted. Beneath the sentence are five lettered words or sets of words. Choose the word or set of words for each blank that best fits the meaning of the sentence as a whole.

1. Created to serve as perfectly as possible their workaday -------, the wooden storage boxes made in America's Shaker communities are now ------- for their beauty.

    (A) environment. .accepted
    (B) owners. .employed
    (C) function. .valued
    (D) reality. .transformed
    (E) image. .seen

2. In order to ------- her theory that the reactions are -------, the scientist conducted many experiments, all of which showed that the heat of the first reaction is more than twice that of the second.

    (A) support. .different
    (B) comprehend. .constant
    (C) evaluate. .concentrated
    (D) capture. .valuable
    (E) demonstrate. .problematic

3. The sheer bulk of data from the mass media seems to overpower us and drive us to ------- accounts for an easily and readily digestible portion of news.

    (A) insular   (B) investigative   (C) synoptic
    (D) subjective   (E) sensational

4. William James lacked the usual ------- death; writing to his dying father, he spoke without ------- about the old man's impending death.

    (A) longing for. .regret
    (B) awe of. .inhibition
    (C) curiosity about. .rancor
    (D) apprehension of. .eloquence
    (E) anticipation of. .commiseration

5. Current data suggest that, although ------- states between fear and aggression exist, fear and aggression are as distinct physiologically as they are psychologically.

    (A) simultaneous
    (B) serious
    (C) exceptional
    (D) partial
    (E) transitional

6. It is ironic that a critic of such overwhelming vanity now suffers from a measure of the oblivion to which he was forever ------- others; in the end, all his ------- has only worked against him.

    (A) dedicating. .self-possession
    (B) leading. .self-righteousness
    (C) consigning. .self-adulation
    (D) relegating. .self-sacrifice
    (E) condemning. .self-analysis

7. Famous among job seekers for its -------, the company, quite apart from generous salaries, bestowed on its executives annual bonuses and such ------- as low-interest home mortgages and company cars.

    (A) magnanimity. .reparations
    (B) inventiveness. .benefits
    (C) largesse. .perquisites
    (D) discernment. .prerogatives
    (E) altruism. .credits

GO ON TO THE NEXT PAGE.

Directions: In each of the following questions, a related pair of words or phrases is followed by five lettered pairs of words or phrases. Select the lettered pair that best expresses a relationship similar to that expressed in the original pair.

8. WEB : SPIDER ::   (A) flower : bee
   (B) canal : otter   (C) nest : bird
    (D) acorn : squirrel   (E) bait : fish

9. FOUR-POSTER : BED ::

   (A) convertible : automobile
   (B) soldier : army
   (C) student : school
   (D) chlorine : water
   (E) paper : wood

10. BONE : BODY ::   (A) scaffold : hinge
    (B) brace : corner   (C) strut : buttress
     (D) lattice : division   (E) girder : skyscraper

11. SCOOP : CONCAVE ::   (A) tongs : hollow
    (B) spatula : flat   (C) beater : tined
     (D) cleaver : indented   (E) skewer : rounded

12. SYMBOLS : REBUS ::

    (A) notes : score
    (B) military : insignia
    (C) proportions : recipe
    (D) program : computer
    (E) silversmith : hallmark

13. GUSH : EFFUSIVE ::

    (A) exult : honest
    (B) deliberate : secretive
    (C) giggle : innocent
    (D) rage : irate
    (E) whisper : confidential

14. PERORATION : SPEECH ::
    (A) tempo : movement   (B) figure : portrait
     (C) light : shadow   (D) verse : stanza
      (E) coda : sonata

15. INTERREGNUM : GOVERNMENT ::
    (A) splice : rope   (B) cleavage : crystal
     (C) infraction : law   (D) frequency : wave
      (E) hibernation : activity

16. EMBROIDER : CLOTH ::

    (A) chase : metal
    (B) patch : quilt
    (C) gild : gold
    (D) carve : knife
    (E) stain : glass

GO ON TO THE NEXT PAGE.

Directions: Each passage in this group is followed by questions based on its content. After reading a passage, choose the best answer to each question. Answer all questions following a passage on the basis of what is <u>stated</u> or <u>implied</u> in that passage.

Visual recognition involves storing and retrieving memories. Neural activity, triggered by the eye, forms an image in the brain's memory system that constitutes an internal representation of the viewed object. When an object is encountered again, it is matched with its internal representation and thereby recognized. Controversy surrounds the question of whether recognition is a parallel, one-step process or a serial, step-by-step one. Psychologists of the Gestalt school maintain that objects are recognized as wholes in a parallel procedure: the internal representation is matched with the retinal image in a single operation. Other psychologists have proposed that internal representation features are matched serially with an object's features. Although some experiments show that, as an object becomes familiar, its internal representation becomes more holistic and the recognition process correspondingly more parallel, the weight of evidence seems to support the serial hypothesis, at least for objects that are not notably simple and familiar.

17. The author is primarily concerned with

   (A) explaining how the brain receives images
   (B) synthesizing hypotheses of visual recognition
   (C) examining the evidence supporting the serial-recognition hypothesis
   (D) discussing visual recognition and some hypotheses proposed to explain it
   (E) reporting on recent experiments dealing with memory systems and their relationship to neural activity

18. According to the passage, Gestalt psychologists make which of the following suppositions about visual recognition?

   I. A retinal image is in exactly the same form as its internal representation.
   II. An object is recognized as a whole without any need for analysis into component parts.
   III. The matching of an object with its internal representation occurs in only one step.

   (A) II only
   (B) III only
   (C) I and III only
   (D) II and III only
   (E) I, II, and III

19. It can be inferred from the passage that the matching process in visual recognition is

   (A) not a neural activity
   (B) not possible when an object is viewed for the very first time
   (C) not possible if a feature of a familiar object is changed in some way
   (D) only possible when a retinal image is received in the brain as a unitary whole
   (E) now fully understood as a combination of the serial and parallel processes

20. In terms of its tone and form, the passage can best be characterized as

   (A) a biased exposition
   (B) a speculative study
   (C) a dispassionate presentation
   (D) an indignant denial
   (E) a dogmatic explanation

GO ON TO THE NEXT PAGE.

In large part as a consequence of the feminist movement, historians have focused a great deal of attention in recent years on determining more accurately the status of women in various periods. Although much has been accomplished for the modern period, premodern cultures have proved more difficult: sources are restricted in number, fragmentary, difficult to interpret, and often contradictory. Thus it is not particularly surprising that some earlier scholarship concerning such cultures has so far gone unchallenged. An example is Johann Bachofen's 1861 treatise on Amazons, women-ruled societies of questionable existence contemporary with ancient Greece.

Starting from the premise that mythology and legend preserve at least a nucleus of historical fact, Bachofen argued that women were dominant in many ancient societies. His work was based on a comprehensive survey of references in the ancient sources to Amazonian and other societies with matrilineal customs—societies in which descent and property rights are traced through the female line. Some support for his theory can be found in evidence such as that drawn from Herodotus, the Greek "historian" of the fifth century B.C., who speaks of an Amazonian society, the Sauromatae, where the women hunted and fought in wars. A woman in this society was not allowed to marry until she had killed a person in battle.

Nonetheless, this assumption that the first recorders of ancient myths have preserved facts is problematic. If one begins by examining why ancients refer to Amazons, it becomes clear that ancient Greek descriptions of such societies were meant not so much to represent observed historical fact—real Amazonian societies—but rather to offer "moral lessons" on the supposed outcome of women's rule in their own society. The Amazons were often characterized, for example, as the equivalents of giants and centaurs, enemies to be slain by Greek heroes. Their customs were presented not as those of a respectable society, but as the very antitheses of ordinary Greek practices.

Thus, I would argue, the purpose of accounts of the Amazons for their male Greek recorders was didactic, to teach both male and female Greeks that all-female groups, formed by withdrawal from traditional society, are destructive and dangerous. Myths about the Amazons were used as arguments for the male-dominated status quo, in which groups composed exclusively of either sex were not permitted to segregate themselves permanently from society. Bachofen was thus misled in his reliance on myths for information about the status of women. The sources that will probably tell contemporary historians most about women in the ancient world are such social documents as gravestones, wills, and marriage contracts. Studies of such documents have already begun to show how mistaken we are when we try to derive our picture of the ancient world exclusively from literary sources, especially myths.

21. The primary purpose of the passage is to

(A) compare competing new approaches to understanding the role of women in ancient societies
(B) investigate the ramifications of Bachofen's theory about the dominance of women in ancient societies
(C) explain the burgeoning interest among historians in determining the actual status of women in various societies
(D) analyze the nature of Amazonian society and uncover similarities between it and the Greek world
(E) criticize the value of ancient myths in determining the status of women in ancient societies

22. All of the following are stated by the author as problems connected with the sources for knowledge of premodern cultures EXCEPT

(A) partial completeness
(B) restricted accessibility
(C) difficulty of interpretation
(D) limited quantity
(E) tendency toward contradiction

23. Which of the following can be inferred from the passage about the myths recorded by the ancient Greeks?

I. They sometimes included portrayals of women holding positions of power.
II. They sometimes contained elaborate explanations of inheritance customs.
III. They comprise almost all of the material available to historians about ancient Greece.

(A) I only   (B) III only   (C) I and III only
(D) II and III only   (E) I, II, and III

GO ON TO THE NEXT PAGE.

24. Which of the following is presented in the passage as evidence supporting the author's view of the ancient Greeks' descriptions of the Amazons?

   (A) The requirement that Sauromatae women kill in battle before marrying
   (B) The failure of historians to verify that women were ever governors of ancient societies
   (C) The classing of Amazons with giants and centaurs
   (D) The well-established unreliability of Herodotus as a source of information about ancient societies
   (E) The recent discovery of ancient societies with matrilineal customs

25. It can be inferred from the passage that the probable reactions of many males in ancient Greece to the idea of a society ruled by women could best be characterized as

   (A) confused and dismayed
   (B) wary and hostile
   (C) cynical and disinterested
   (D) curious but fearful
   (E) excited but anxious

26. The author suggests that the main reason for the persisting influence of Bachofen's work is that

   (A) feminists have shown little interest in ancient societies
   (B) Bachofen's knowledge of Amazonian culture is unparalleled
   (C) reliable information about the ancient world is difficult to acquire
   (D) ancient societies show the best evidence of women in positions of power
   (E) historians have been primarily interested in the modern period

27. The author's attitude toward Bachofen's treatise is best described as one of

   (A) qualified approval
   (B) profound ambivalence
   (C) studied neutrality
   (D) pointed disagreement
   (E) unmitigated hostility

GO ON TO THE NEXT PAGE.

Directions: Each question below consists of a word printed in capital letters, followed by five lettered words or phrases. Choose the lettered word or phrase that is most nearly opposite in meaning to the word in capital letters.

Since some of the questions require you to distinguish fine shades of meaning, be sure to consider all the choices before deciding which one is best.

28. COLLECT : (A) scatter   (B) avoid
    (C) hide   (D) search   (E) create

29. SERRATED : (A) without joints
    (B) without folds   (C) without notches
    (D) variegated   (E) mutated

30. FLEDGLING :
    (A) experienced practitioner
    (B) successful competitor
    (C) reluctant volunteer
    (D) recent convert
    (E) attentive listener

31. SUPPOSITION :
    (A) certainty
    (B) inferiority
    (C) irrelevance
    (D) unexpected occurrence
    (E) clear position

32. ABERRANT : (A) attractive   (B) predictive
    (C) blissful   (D) normal   (E) precise

33. OBDURATE : (A) flexible
    (B) timid   (C) retrospective
    (D) whimsical   (E) alienated

34. LIST : (A) be upside down
    (B) be upright   (C) slide backward
    (D) sway to and fro   (E) lie flat

35. FORESTALL : (A) announce
    (B) equivocate   (C) prolong
    (D) precipitate   (E) steady

36. TENDENTIOUS : (A) unbiased
    (B) severely hampered   (C) inapplicable
    (D) highly productive   (E) curved

37. REDUNDANT : (A) consistent
    (B) complex   (C) diffuse
    (D) insightful   (E) economical

38. RUE : (A) tenderness   (B) sincerity
    (C) heartiness   (D) spite   (E) satisfaction

S T O P

IF YOU FINISH BEFORE TIME IS CALLED, YOU MAY CHECK YOUR WORK ON THIS SECTION ONLY.
DO NOT WORK ON ANY OTHER SECTION IN THE TEST.

Section 2 starts on page 77.

SECTION 2

Time—30 minutes

38 Questions

Directions: Each sentence below has one or two blanks, each blank indicating that something has been omitted. Beneath the sentence are five lettered words or sets of words. Choose the word or set of words for each blank that best fits the meaning of the sentence as a whole.

1. There are no solitary, free-living creatures; every form of life is ------- other forms.

   (A) segregated from   (B) parallel to
   (C) dependent on   (D) overshadowed by
   (E) mimicked by

2. The sale of Alaska was not so much an American coup as a matter of ------- for an imperial Russia that was short of cash and unable to ------- its own continental coastline.

   (A) negligence. .fortify
   (B) custom. .maintain
   (C) convenience. .stabilize
   (D) expediency. .defend
   (E) exigency. .reinforce

3. Despite assorted effusions to the contrary, there is no necessary link between scientific skill and humanism, and, quite possibly, there may be something of a ------- between them.

   (A) generality   (B) fusion   (C) congruity
   (D) dichotomy   (E) reciprocity

4. A common argument claims that in folk art, the artist's subordination of technical mastery to intense feeling ------- the direct communication of emotion to the viewer.

   (A) facilitates   (B) averts   (C) neutralizes
   (D) implies   (E) represses

5. While not completely nonplussed by the unusually caustic responses from members of the audience, the speaker was nonetheless visibly ------- by their lively criticism.

   (A) humiliated
   (B) discomfited
   (C) deluded
   (D) disgraced
   (E) tantalized

6. In eighth-century Japan, people who ------- wasteland were rewarded with official ranks as part of an effort to overcome the shortage of ------- fields.

   (A) conserved. .forested
   (B) reclaimed. .arable
   (C) cultivated. .domestic
   (D) irrigated. .accessible
   (E) located. .desirable

7. If duty is the natural ------- of one's ------- the course of future events, then people who are powerful have duty placed on them whether they like it or not.

   (A) correlate. .understanding of
   (B) outgrowth. .control over
   (C) determinant. .involvement in
   (D) mitigant. .preoccupation with
   (E) arbiter. .responsibility for

GO ON TO THE NEXT PAGE.

Directions: In each of the following questions, a related pair of words or phrases is followed by five lettered pairs of words or phrases. Select the lettered pair that best expresses a relationship similar to that expressed in the original pair.

8. COMA : UNCONSCIOUSNESS ::
   (A) amnesia : effort
   (B) delirium : confusion
   (C) paralysis : pain
   (D) hallucination : numbness
   (E) fever : calm

9. TOURNIQUET : BLOOD ::   (A) bridge : river
   (B) antiseptic : surgery   (C) dam : water
    (D) pressure : air   (E) bucket : well

10. FOUNDATION : HOUSE ::
    (A) mountain : tunnel
    (B) ground : sky
    (C) net : trapeze
    (D) pedestal : statue
    (E) pole : banner

11. PHILATELIST : STAMPS ::
    (A) numismatist : coins
    (B) astrologer : predictions
    (C) geneticist : chromosomes
    (D) cartographer : maps
    (E) pawnbroker : jewelry

12. INSECT : BUTTERFLY ::
    (A) perfume : essence
    (B) botany : chrysanthemum
    (C) philosophy : metaphysics
    (D) pitch : black
    (E) color : brightness

13. PERNICIOUS : INJURE ::
    (A) officious : deny
    (B) propitious : conjure
    (C) audacious : allude
    (D) avaricious : dispel
    (E) disingenuous : mislead

14. FLAG : VIGOR ::   (A) endure : courage
    (B) tire : monotony   (C) question : perception
     (D) waver : resolution   (E) flatter : charm

15. EMBARRASS : MORTIFY ::
    (A) adumbrate : insinuate
    (B) indulge : mollycoddle
    (C) aggrandize : venerate
    (D) relent : deflate
    (E) upstage : demoralize

16. DISTILL : PURITY ::
    (A) leaven : volume
    (B) pulverize : fragility
    (C) absorb : brilliance
    (D) homogenize : fluidity
    (E) conduct : charge

GO ON TO THE NEXT PAGE.

Directions: Each passage in this group is followed by questions based on its content. After reading a passage, choose the best answer to each question. Answer all questions following a passage on the basis of what is stated or implied in that passage.

Initially the Vinaver theory that Malory's eight romances, once thought to be fundamentally unified, were in fact eight independent works produced both a sense of relief and an unpleasant shock. Vinaver's theory comfortably explained away the apparent contradictions of chronology and made each romance independently satisfying. It was, however, disagreeable to find that what had been thought of as one book was now eight books. Part of this response was the natural reaction to the disturbance of set ideas. Nevertheless, even now, after lengthy consideration of the theory's refined but legitimate observations, one cannot avoid the conclusion that the eight romances are only one work. It is not quite a matter of disagreeing with the theory of independence, but of rejecting its implications: that the romances may be taken in any or no particular order, that they have no cumulative effect, and that they are as separate as the works of a modern novelist.

17. The primary purpose of the passage is to

(A) discuss the validity of a hypothesis
(B) summarize a system of general principles
(C) propose guidelines for future argument
(D) stipulate conditions for acceptance of an interpretation
(E) deny accusations about an apparent contradiction

18. It can be inferred from the passage that the author believes which of the following about Malory's works?

I. There are meaningful links between and among the romances.
II. The subtleties of the romances are obscured when they are taken as one work.
III. Any contradictions in chronology among the romances are less important than their overall unity.

(A) I only
(B) III only
(C) I and III only
(D) II and III only
(E) I, II, and III

19. The author of the passage concedes which of the following about the Vinaver theory?

(A) It gives a clearer understanding of the unity of Malory's romances.
(B) It demonstrates the irrationality of considering Malory's romances to be unified.
(C) It establishes acceptable links between Malory's romances and modern novels.
(D) It unifies earlier and later theories concerning the chronology of Malory's romances.
(E) It makes valid and subtle comments about Malory's romances.

20. It can be inferred from the passage that, in evaluating the Vinaver theory, some critics were

(A) frequently misled by the inconsistencies in Malory's work
(B) initially biased by previous interpretations of Malory's work
(C) conceptually displeased by the general interpretation that Vinaver rejected
(D) generally in agreement with Vinaver's comparisons between Malory and modern novelists
(E) originally skeptical about Vinaver's early conclusions with respect to modern novels

GO ON TO THE NEXT PAGE.

We can distinguish three different realms of matter, three levels on the quantum ladder. The first is the atomic realm, which includes the world of atoms, their interactions, and the structures that are formed by them, such as molecules, liquids and solids, and gases and plasmas. This realm includes all the phenomena of atomic physics, chemistry, and, in a certain sense, biology. The energy exchanges taking place in this realm are of a relatively low order. If these exchanges are below one electron volt, such as in the collisions between molecules of the air in a room, then atoms and molecules can be regarded as elementary particles. That is, they have "conditional elementarity" because they keep their identity and do not change in any collisions or in other processes at these low energy exchanges. If one goes to higher energy exchanges, say 10^4 electron volts, then atoms and molecules will decompose into nuclei and electrons; at this level, the latter particles must be considered as elementary. We find examples of structures and processes of this first rung of the quantum ladder on Earth, on planets, and on the surfaces of stars.

The next rung is the nuclear realm. Here the energy exchanges are much higher, on the order of millions of electron volts. As long as we are dealing with phenomena in the atomic realm, such amounts of energy are unavailable, and most nuclei are inert: they do not change. However, if one applies energies of millions of electron volts, nuclear reactions, fission and fusion, and the processes of radioactivity occur; our elementary particles then are protons, neutrons, and electrons. In addition, nuclear processes produce neutrinos, particles that have no detectable mass or charge. In the universe, energies at this level are available in the centers of stars and in star explosions. Indeed, the energy radiated by the stars is produced by nuclear reactions. The natural radioactivity we find on Earth is the long-lived remnant of the time when now-earthly matter was expelled into space by a major stellar explosion.

The third rung of the quantum ladder is the subnuclear realm. Here we are dealing with energy exchanges of many billions of electron volts. We encounter excited nucleons, new types of particles such as mesons, heavy electrons, quarks, and gluons, and also antimatter in large quantities. The gluons are the quanta, or smallest units, of the force (the strong force) that keeps the quarks together. As long as we are dealing with the atomic or nuclear realm, these new types of particles do not occur and the nucleons remain inert. But at subnuclear energy levels, the nucleons and mesons appear to be composed of quarks, so that the quarks and gluons figure as elementary particles.

21. The primary topic of the passage is which of the following?

    (A) The interaction of the realms on the quantum ladder
    (B) Atomic structures found on Earth, on other planets, and on the surfaces of stars
    (C) Levels of energy that are released in nuclear reactions on Earth and in stars
    (D) Particles and processes found in the atomic, nuclear, and subnuclear realms
    (E) New types of particles occurring in the atomic realm

GO ON TO THE NEXT PAGE.

22. According to the passage, radioactivity that occurs naturally on Earth is the result of

(A) the production of particles that have no detectable mass or electric charge
(B) high energy exchanges on the nuclear level that occurred in an ancient explosion in a star
(C) processes that occur in the center of the Sun, which emits radiation to the Earth
(D) phenomena in the atomic realm that cause atoms and molecules to decompose into nuclei and electrons
(E) high-voltage discharges of electricity that took place in the atmosphere of the Earth shortly after the Earth was formed

23. The author organizes the passage by

(A) making distinctions between two groups of particles, those that are elementary and those that are composite
(B) explaining three methods of transferring energy to atoms and to the smaller particles that constitute atoms
(C) describing several levels of processes, increasing in energy, and corresponding sets of particles, generally decreasing in size
(D) putting forth an argument concerning energy levels and then conceding that several qualifications of that argument are necessary
(E) making several successive refinements of a definition of elementarity on the basis of several groups of experimental results

24. According to the passage, which of the following can be found in the atomic realm?

(A) More than one level of energy exchange
(B) Exactly one elementary particle
(C) Exactly three kinds of atomic structures
(D) Three levels on the quantum ladder
(E) No particles smaller than atoms

25. According to the author, gluons are not

(A) considered to be detectable
(B) produced in nuclear reactions
(C) encountered in subnuclear energy exchanges
(D) related to the strong force
(E) found to be conditionally elementary

26. At a higher energy level than the subnuclear level described, if such a higher level exists, it can be expected on the basis of the information in the passage that there would probably be

(A) excited nucleons
(B) elementary mesons
(C) a kind of particle without detectable mass or charge
(D) exchanges of energy on the order of millions of electron volts
(E) another set of elementary particles

27. The passage speaks of particles as having conditional elementarity if they

(A) remain unchanged at a given level of energy exchange
(B) cannot be decomposed into smaller constituents
(C) are mathematically simpler than some other set of particles
(D) release energy at a low level in collisions
(E) belong to the nuclear level on the quantum ladder

GO ON TO THE NEXT PAGE.

Directions: Each question below consists of a word printed in capital letters, followed by five lettered words or phrases. Choose the lettered word or phrase that is most nearly <u>opposite</u> in meaning to the word in capital letters.

Since some of the questions require you to distinguish fine shades of meaning, be sure to consider all the choices before deciding which one is best.

28. PARTITION: (A) unify   (B) mollify
    (C) nullify   (D) indemnify   (E) fortify

29. ABHOR: (A) greatly admire
    (B) promise absolutely   (C) inspire
    (D) credit   (E) improve

30. TAINTED: (A) available   (B) strident
    (C) conspicuous   (D) wholesome
    (E) insensible

31. CARDINAL: (A) abstract   (B) elusive
    (C) subtle   (D) minor   (E) miniature

32. ESTRANGEMENT:
    (A) reconciliation   (B) dissemblance
    (C) consolation   (D) chaotic situation
    (E) continuous negotiation

33. ABATE: (A) attach   (B) alter
    (C) absent   (D) assist   (E) augment

34. DOFF: (A) raze   (B) don   (C) ply
    (D) clasp tightly   (E) hide carefully

35. ERUDITE: (A) unsettled
    (B) unfettered   (C) untalented
    (D) untitled   (E) unlettered

36. GARRULITY: (A) servility
    (B) forbearance   (C) peacefulness
    (D) constancy   (E) taciturnity

37. SCOTCH: (A) entrust   (B) emphasize
    (C) encourage   (D) renovate
    (E) unfasten

38. LIBERTINE: (A) serf   (B) miser
    (C) prisoner   (D) ascetic
    (E) authoritarian

S T O P

**IF YOU FINISH BEFORE TIME IS CALLED, YOU MAY CHECK YOUR WORK ON THIS SECTION ONLY.
DO NOT WORK ON ANY OTHER SECTION IN THE TEST.**

Section 3 starts on page 84.

SECTION 3
Time—30 minutes

30 Questions

Numbers: All numbers used are real numbers.

Figures: Position of points, angles, regions, etc. can be assumed to be in the order shown; and angle measures can be assumed to be positive.

Lines shown as straight can be assumed to be straight.

Figures can be assumed to lie in a plane unless otherwise indicated.

Figures that accompany questions are intended to provide information useful in answering the questions. However, unless a note states that a figure is drawn to scale, you should solve these problems NOT by estimating sizes by sight or by measurement, but by using your knowledge of mathematics (see Example 2 below).

Directions: Each of the Questions 1-15 consists of two quantities, one in Column A and one in Column B. You are to compare the two quantities and choose

    A if the quantity in Column A is greater;
    B if the quantity in Column B is greater;
    C if the two quantities are equal;
    D if the relationship cannot be determined from the information given.

Note: Since there are only four choices, NEVER MARK (E).

Common
Information: In a question, information concerning one or both of the quantities to be compared is centered above the two columns. A symbol that appears in both columns represents the same thing in Column A as it does in Column B.

	Column A	Column B	Sample Answers
Example 1:	2×6	$2 + 6$	● Ⓑ Ⓒ Ⓓ Ⓔ

Examples 2-4 refer to $\triangle PQR$.

$$\begin{array}{c} R \\ x° \\ y° \\ w° \; z° \\ P \qquad N \qquad Q \end{array}$$

			Sample Answers
Example 2:	PN	NQ	Ⓐ Ⓑ Ⓒ ● Ⓔ

(since equal measures cannot be assumed, even though PN and NQ appear equal)

Example 3:	x	y	Ⓐ ● Ⓒ Ⓓ Ⓔ

(since N is between P and Q)

Example 4:	$w + z$	180	Ⓐ Ⓑ ● Ⓓ Ⓔ

(since PQ is a straight line)

GO ON TO THE NEXT PAGE.

A if the quantity in Column A is greater;
B if the quantity in Column B is greater;
C if the two quantities are equal;
D if the relationship cannot be determined from the information given.

Column A	Column B

1. The cost of 3 pounds of peaches at $0.34 per pound   — $1.00

2. $\dfrac{3}{4} - \dfrac{2}{3}$ — $\dfrac{1}{12}$

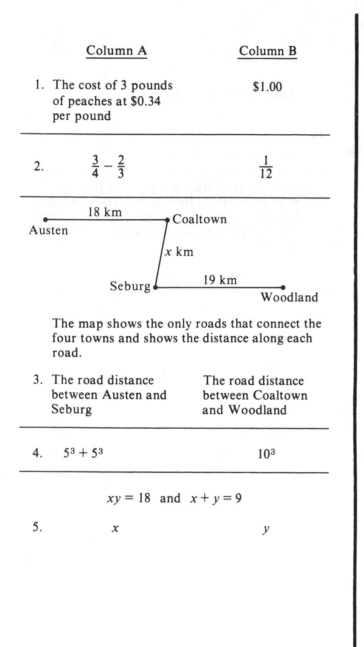

The map shows the only roads that connect the four towns and shows the distance along each road.

3. The road distance between Austen and Seburg   —   The road distance between Coaltown and Woodland

4. $5^3 + 5^3$ — 10^3

$xy = 18$ and $x + y = 9$

5. x — y

Column A	Column B

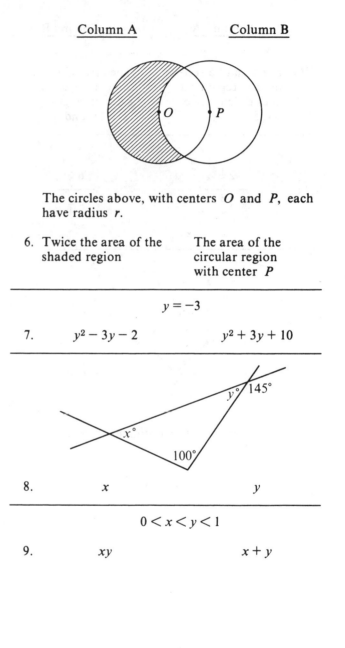

The circles above, with centers O and P, each have radius r.

6. Twice the area of the shaded region   —   The area of the circular region with center P

$y = -3$

7. $y^2 - 3y - 2$ — $y^2 + 3y + 10$

8. x — y

$0 < x < y < 1$

9. xy — $x + y$

GO ON TO THE NEXT PAGE.

A if the quantity in Column A is greater;
B if the quantity in Column B is greater;
C if the two quantities are equal;
D if the relationship cannot be determined from the information given.

Column A	Column B

10. The area of a rectangular region with sides of lengths a and 5 | The area of a rectangular region with sides of lengths $(a + 1)$ and 4

11. $\dfrac{2\frac{1}{2}}{3\frac{3}{4}}$ $\dfrac{6\frac{1}{2}}{9\frac{3}{4}}$

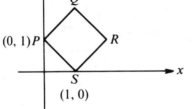

In the rectangular coordinate system above, *PQRS* is a square.

12. The perimeter of *PQRS*   4

Column A	Column B

When integer n is divided by 9, the remainder is 2.

13. The remainder when n is divided by 3   2

A certain store sells each pencil at the same price regardless of the number of pencils sold. k of these pencils have a total price of q cents, and r of these pencils have a total price of s cents.

14. ks qr

15. $a^2 + b^2$ $(a + b)^2$

GO ON TO THE NEXT PAGE.

Directions: Each of the Questions 16-30 has five answer choices. For each of these questions, select the best of the answer choices given.

16. On a number line, what is the distance between −3 and 7 ?

    (A) 10   (B) 8   (C) 7   (D) 5   (E) 4

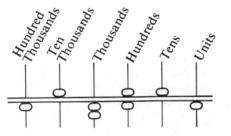

17. In the figure above, each of the beads above the horizontal bar represents 5 times the place value indicated and each of the beads below the bar represents 1 times the place value indicated. What number is represented by the figure above?

    (A) 512,651
    (B) 512,615
    (C) 156,651
    (D) 152,651
    (E) 152,251

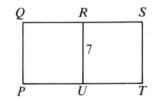

18. In the figure above, if *PQRU* and *URST* are squares, what is the area of rectangular region *PQST* ?

    (A) 28   (B) 42   (C) 49   (D) 98

    (E) It cannot be determined from the information given.

19. Each of the following is the square of an integer EXCEPT

    (A) 81   (B) 100   (C) 121
    (D) 196   (E) 215

20. The average (arithmetic mean) of two numbers is $2x + 1$. If one of the numbers is x, then the other number is

    (A) $x - 1$
    (B) $x + 1$
    (C) $2x - 1$
    (D) $3x + 1$
    (E) $3x + 2$

GO ON TO THE NEXT PAGE.

Questions 21-25 refer to the following graph.

RESULTS OF A SAMPLE OF VOTERS
IN DISTRICT X

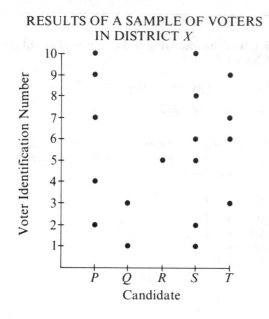

The graph above shows how a sample of 10 different voters (vertical axis) voted for 5 different candidates (horizontal axis). Each voter voted for either one or two of the five candidates. (No voter voted twice for the same candidate.) The two candidates receiving the most votes were the winners. The sample constituted 5 percent of those in the district who voted, and the number of votes in the district for each candidate was in the same proportion as the number of votes in the sample for each candidate.

21. How many people in the sample voted for both winners?

   (A) One
   (B) Two
   (C) Three
   (D) Five
   (E) Six

22. What fraction of the total number of votes cast did the two winners receive?

   (A) $\frac{11}{18}$ (B) $\frac{11}{20}$ (C) $\frac{1}{2}$ (D) $\frac{1}{3}$ (E) $\frac{3}{10}$

23. What percent of the sample voted for at least one of the two winners?

   (A) 11%
   (B) 20%
   (C) 55%
   (D) 61%
   (E) 90%

24. How many votes were cast in district X?

   (A) 18   (B) 90   (C) 200
   (D) 360   (E) 400

25. In district X, candidate T received how many more votes than candidate Q?

   (A) 2   (B) 10   (C) 20   (D) 40   (E) 80

GO ON TO THE NEXT PAGE.

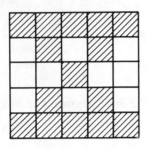

26. In the figure above, the number of shaded squares is what percent greater than the number of unshaded squares?

    (A) 25%   (B) 40%   (C) 50%
    (D) 60%   (E) 75%

27. If x, y, and z are three different positive integers less than 10, what is the greatest possible value of the expression $\frac{x-y}{z}$?

    (A) 8
    (B) 7
    (C) 6
    (D) 5
    (E) 4

29. If p is a prime number greater than 11, and p is the sum of the two prime numbers x and y, then x could be which of the following?

    (A) 2   (B) 5   (C) 7   (D) 9   (E) 13

30. If 18 identical machines required 40 days to complete a job, how many fewer days would have been required to do the job if 6 additional machines of the same type had been used from the beginning?

    (A) 10

    (B) $13\frac{1}{3}$

    (C) 16

    (D) $26\frac{2}{3}$

    (E) 36

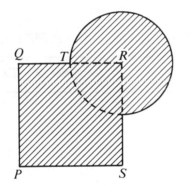

28. In the figure above, vertex R of square $PQRS$ is the center of the circle. If $QT = TR = 3$, what is the area of the shaded region?

    (A) $9 + \frac{27}{4}\pi$

    (B) $9 + 27\pi$

    (C) $36 + \frac{27}{4}\pi$

    (D) $36 + 9\pi$

    (E) $36 + 27\pi$

S T O P

IF YOU FINISH BEFORE TIME IS CALLED, YOU MAY CHECK YOUR WORK ON THIS SECTION ONLY.
DO NOT WORK ON ANY OTHER SECTION IN THE TEST.

SECTION 4
Time—30 minutes
30 Questions

Numbers: All numbers used are real numbers.

Figures: Position of points, angles, regions, etc. can be assumed to be in the order shown; and angle measures can be assumed to be positive.

Lines shown as straight can be assumed to be straight.

Figures can be assumed to lie in a plane unless otherwise indicated.

Figures that accompany questions are intended to provide information useful in answering the questions. However, unless a note states that a figure is drawn to scale, you should solve these problems NOT by estimating sizes by sight or by measurement, but by using your knowledge of mathematics (see Example 2 below).

Directions: Each of the <u>Questions 1-15</u> consists of two quantities, one in Column A and one in Column B. You are to compare the two quantities and choose

A if the quantity in Column A is greater;
B if the quantity in Column B is greater;
C if the two quantities are equal;
D if the relationship cannot be determined from the information given.

Note: Since there are only four choices, **NEVER MARK (E)**.

Common Information: In a question, information concerning one or both of the quantities to be compared is centered above the two columns. A symbol that appears in both columns represents the same thing in Column A as it does in Column B.

	Column A	Column B	Sample Answers
Example 1:	2×6	$2 + 6$	● Ⓑ Ⓒ Ⓓ Ⓔ

Examples 2-4 refer to $\triangle PQR$.

	Column A	Column B	Sample Answers
Example 2:	PN	NQ	Ⓐ Ⓑ Ⓒ ● Ⓔ

(since equal measures cannot be assumed, even though PN and NQ appear equal)

Example 3:	x	y	Ⓐ ● Ⓒ Ⓓ Ⓔ

(since N is between P and Q)

Example 4:	$w + z$	180	Ⓐ Ⓑ ● Ⓓ Ⓔ

(since PQ is a straight line)

GO ON TO THE NEXT PAGE.

A if the quantity in Column A is greater;
B if the quantity in Column B is greater;
C if the two quantities are equal;
D if the relationship cannot be determined from the information given.

Column A   Column B

1. The least common   15
   denominator of
   $\frac{1}{2}$, $\frac{1}{3}$, and $\frac{1}{4}$

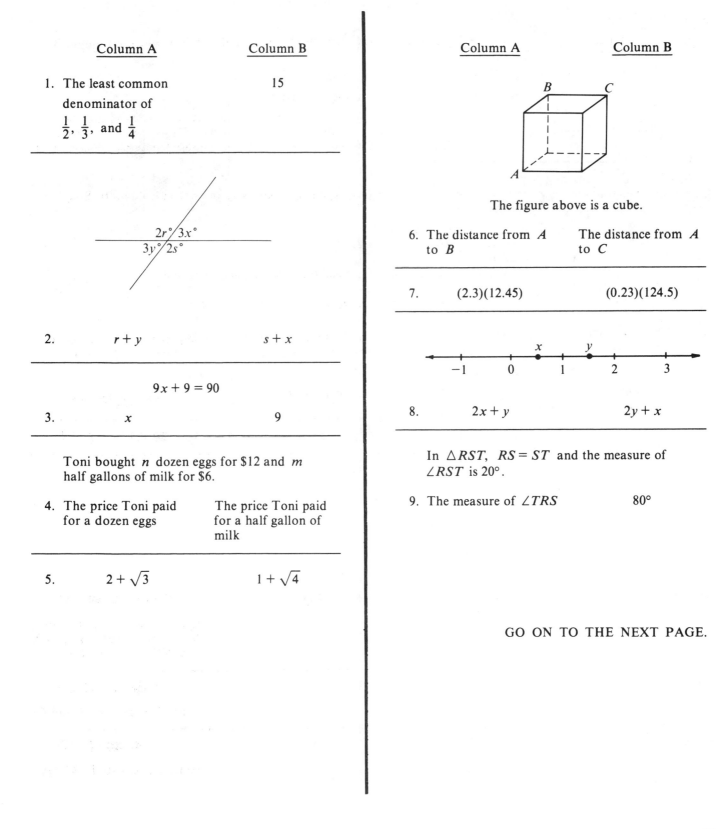

2. $r + y$ $s + x$

$9x + 9 = 90$

3. x 9

Toni bought n dozen eggs for $12 and m
half gallons of milk for $6.

4. The price Toni paid   The price Toni paid
   for a dozen eggs   for a half gallon of
                          milk

5. $2 + \sqrt{3}$ $1 + \sqrt{4}$

Column A   Column B

The figure above is a cube.

6. The distance from A The distance from A
   to B to C

7. $(2.3)(12.45)$ $(0.23)(124.5)$

8. $2x + y$ $2y + x$

In $\triangle RST$, $RS = ST$ and the measure of
$\angle RST$ is $20°$.

9. The measure of $\angle TRS$ $80°$

GO ON TO THE NEXT PAGE.

91

A   if the quantity in Column A is greater;
B   if the quantity in Column B is greater;
C   if the two quantities are equal;
D   if the relationship cannot be determined from the information given.

Column A	Column B

x and *y* are positive numbers.

10. $\left(\dfrac{x+y}{2}\right)^2 - \left(\dfrac{x-y}{2}\right)^2$ 0

The diameter of the semicircle is 12 and the height of the triangle is 8.

11. The area of the semi-circular region   The area of triangular region *PQR*

Fahrenheit temperatures recorded at location *X* at 4-hour intervals were $-8°$, $-5°$, $7°$, $5°$, $3°$, $1°$.

12. The average (arithmetic mean) of the temperatures recorded above $1°$ F

Column A	Column B

The diagram represents a rectangular garden. The shaded regions are planted in flowers, and the unshaded region is a walk 2 feet wide. All angles are right angles.

13. The sum of the areas of the shaded regions   2,800 square feet

---

14. 8^7 $8^6 + 2\cdot 8^6 + 4\cdot 8^6$

$x \neq 0$

15. $\dfrac{19}{20}x$ $\dfrac{20}{19}\left(\dfrac{1}{x}\right)$

GO ON TO THE NEXT PAGE.

Directions: Each of the Questions 16-30 has five answer choices. For each of these questions, select the best of the answer choices given.

16. If $a = 3b + c$, what is the value of b when $a = 17$ and $c = 2$?

(A) 5

(B) $6\frac{1}{3}$

(C) 12

(D) 15

(E) 45

17. $\dfrac{\frac{1}{3}}{6} =$

(A) 2 (B) $\frac{1}{2}$ (C) $\frac{1}{3}$ (D) $\frac{1}{9}$ (E) $\frac{1}{18}$

18. If $4x - 2y = 8$, what is the value of $2x - y$?

(A) 3 (B) 4 (C) 5 (D) 6

(E) It cannot be determined from the information given.

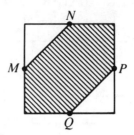

19. In the square above, M, N, P, and Q are midpoints of the sides. If the area of the square region is A, what is the area of the shaded region?

(A) $\frac{1}{3} A$

(B) $\frac{1}{2} A$

(C) $\frac{2}{3} A$

(D) $\frac{3}{4} A$

(E) $\frac{7}{8} A$

20. What is the least number x for which $(2x + 1)(x - 2) = 0$?

(A) -2 (B) -1 (C) $-\frac{1}{2}$ (D) $\frac{1}{2}$ (E) 2

GO ON TO THE NEXT PAGE.

Questions 21-25 refer to the following graphs.

FEDERAL BUDGET OUTLAYS OF THE UNITED STATES FOR MILITARY EXPENDITURES, 1966-1979

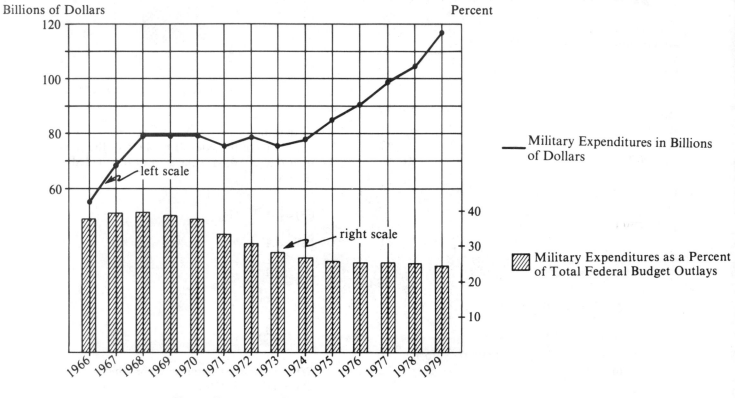

Note: Drawn to scale.

WORLDWIDE MILITARY EXPENDITURES: 1968 TO 1977

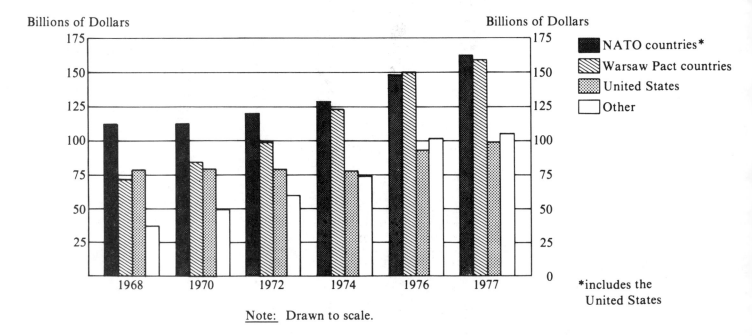

Note: Drawn to scale.

GO ON TO THE NEXT PAGE.

21. In 1968 the military expenditures of the United States were approximately how many billion dollars?

    (A) 100   (B) 80   (C) 70   (D) 60   (E) 40

22. For the year in which the United States had approximately 70 billion dollars in military expenditures, that amount was approximately what percent of total federal budget outlays?

    (A) 30%
    (B) 40%
    (C) 50%
    (D) 60%
    (E) 70%

23. In which of the following years was the amount of United States military expenditures approximately 80 percent of the amount for 1978 ?

    (A) 1967   (B) 1968   (C) 1973
    (D) 1975   (E) 1976

24. In 1977, federal budget outlays for the United States totaled approximately how many billion dollars?

    (A) 200
    (B) 300
    (C) 400
    (D) 500
    (E) 600

25. In which of the years shown were combined military expenditures for the NATO countries other than the United States most nearly equal to 50 billion dollars?

    (A) 1968   (B) 1972   (C) 1974
    (D) 1976   (E) 1977

GO ON TO THE NEXT PAGE.

26. In a certain club for men and women, 40 percent of the members are men. If 20 percent of the men and 10 percent of the women members went to a theater performance, what percent of the total membership went to the performance?

    (A) 12%   (B) 14%   (C) 15%
    (D) 16%   (E) 30%

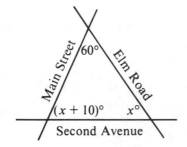

Second Avenue

27. The figure above shows the angles of intersection of three streets. At what angle do Second Avenue and Main Street intersect?

    (A) 50°
    (B) 55°
    (C) 65°
    (D) 70°
    (E) 75°

28. If x, y, and z are consecutive integers and $x < y < z$, which of the following must be true?

    I. xyz is even.
    II. $x + y + z$ is even.
    III. $(x + y)(y + z)$ is odd.

    (A) None
    (B) I only
    (C) II only
    (D) I and III only
    (E) I, II, and III

GO ON TO THE NEXT PAGE.

29. If $<n> = \dfrac{n(n+1)}{2}$ for all integers n, and

$m = <5>$, then $<m> =$

(A) 120
(B) 225
(C) 240
(D) 420
(E) 840

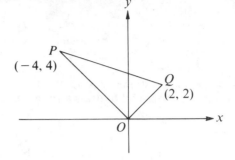

30. In the figure above, what is the perimeter of triangle OPQ?

(A) $4 + 2\sqrt{2}$
(B) $8 + 4\sqrt{2}$
(C) $6 + 2\sqrt{5}$
(D) $6 + 6\sqrt{2}$
(E) $6\sqrt{2} + 2\sqrt{10}$

S T O P

IF YOU FINISH BEFORE TIME IS CALLED, YOU MAY CHECK YOUR WORK ON THIS SECTION ONLY.
DO NOT WORK ON ANY OTHER SECTION IN THE TEST.

5

Time—30 minutes

25 Questions

Directions: Each question or group of questions is based on a passage or set of conditions. In answering some of the questions, it may be useful to draw a rough diagram. For each question, select the best answer choice given.

Questions 1-6

Five ships—J, K, L, M, and N—are to be unloaded on 5 consecutive days beginning on Monday and ending on Friday according to the following conditions:

Each ship takes exactly one day to unload.
K must be unloaded on a day preceding the days M and N are unloaded.
L cannot be unloaded on a Tuesday.
M must be the second ship unloaded after J is unloaded.

1. If M is unloaded on Friday, which of the following must be true?

(A) J is unloaded on Wednesday.
(B) K is unloaded on Tuesday.
(C) L is unloaded on Monday.
(D) L is unloaded on Thursday.
(E) N is unloaded on Thursday.

2. If K, M, and N are to be unloaded one immediately after the other in that order, the two days on which J can be unloaded are

(A) Monday and Tuesday
(B) Monday and Friday
(C) Tuesday and Wednesday
(D) Wednesday and Friday
(E) Thursday and Friday

3. If L is unloaded on the day immediately after the day J is unloaded, which of the following must be true?

(A) J is unloaded on Wednesday.
(B) K is unloaded on Monday.
(C) L is unloaded on Thursday.
(D) M is unloaded on Friday.
(E) N is unloaded on Tuesday.

4. If J is unloaded on Monday, which of the following must be true?

(A) L is unloaded before K.
(B) L is unloaded before M.
(C) K is unloaded on Tuesday.
(D) L is unloaded on Thursday.
(E) N is unloaded on Thursday.

5. N can be unloaded any day of the week EXCEPT

(A) Monday
(B) Tuesday
(C) Wednesday
(D) Thursday
(E) Friday

6. On which of the following days can any one of the five ships be unloaded?

(A) Monday
(B) Tuesday
(C) Wednesday
(D) Thursday
(E) Friday

GO ON TO THE NEXT PAGE.

7. Infection is the biggest threat to the life of a burn patient. The skin, the body's natural barrier against bacteria, is damaged or gone in the burned areas. The bacteria that are a threat are unpredictable in both variety and number. Moreover, those found affecting any one patient may change completely from one day to the next. The standard treatment, therefore, is the administration of broad-spectrum antibiotics.

Considering only the information given about burn patients in the passage above, which of the following is most likely to enhance the effectiveness of the standard treatment of a burn patient?

(A) Keeping the patient in an air-conditioned room until recovery is assured
(B) Keeping the areas affected by burns as dry as possible
(C) Continuously monitoring the patient's vital signs with electronic equipment
(D) Feeding the patient a diet extra rich in calories
(E) Keeping the patient in a maximally sterile environment

8. Dormitories range from two to six stories in height. If a dormitory room is above the second floor, it has a fire escape.

If the statements above are true, which of the following must also be true?

(A) Second-floor dormitory rooms do not have fire escapes.
(B) Third-floor dormitory rooms do not have fire escapes.
(C) Only dormitory rooms above the second floor have fire escapes.
(D) Fourth-floor dormitory rooms have fire escapes.
(E) Some two-story dormitories do not have fire escapes.

9. The garment industry is labor-intensive; the production of garments requires the employment of a relatively large number of people. The auto industry is capital-intensive; a large amount of money is invested in elaborate equipment run by a relatively small number of people. If fringe benefits are not considered, a typical United States garment worker in 1979 earned 46 percent of a typical auto worker's wages.

Which of the following, if true, is likely to be among the factors that account for the disparity between auto workers' and garment workers' wages?

(A) There is generally less variation among the wages of garment industry workers than among those of auto industry workers.
(B) Wage increases in the auto industry have a smaller effect on manufacturers' total costs than do wage increases in the garment industry.
(C) The fringe benefits that auto makers provide for their employees are more comprehensive than are those provided for garment workers.
(D) The auto industry faces more competition from companies outside the United States paying low wages than does the garment industry.
(E) The auto industry employs a larger total number of workers than does the garment industry.

GO ON TO THE NEXT PAGE.

5

Exactly twelve books are arranged from left to right on a shelf.

Of the twelve books, four are small paperback books, two are large paperback books, three are clothbound books, and three are leather-bound books.

The four small paperback books are next to each other, and the three leather-bound books are next to each other.

The first (leftmost) book and the twelfth (rightmost) book are paperback books.

10. If the third book is a small paperback book and each large paperback book is next to a leather-bound book, which of the following books must be a large paperback book?

    (A) The first
    (B) The second
    (C) The sixth
    (D) The eighth
    (E) The eleventh

11. If the twelfth book is a small paperback book, the fourth book is a leather-bound book, and no cloth-bound book is next to another clothbound book, which of the following books must be a large paperback book?

    (A) The second
    (B) The third
    (C) The fifth
    (D) The sixth
    (E) The seventh

12. If the first book is a small paperback book, the clothbound books are next to each other, and the eleventh book is leather bound, which of the following books can be a large paperback book?

    (A) The fourth
    (B) The fifth
    (C) The sixth
    (D) The ninth
    (E) The tenth

13. If the first book is a large paperback book, the second book is a small paperback book, and the seventh book is a leather-bound book, which of the following can be true?

    (A) The fourth book is a clothbound book.
    (B) The fifth book is a leather-bound book.
    (C) The sixth book is a large paperback book.
    (D) The eighth book is a clothbound book.
    (E) The ninth book is a clothbound book.

14. If a large paperback book is at each end of the row and a small paperback book is next to a leather-bound book, which of the following books can be a clothbound book?

    (A) The fourth
    (B) The fifth
    (C) The sixth
    (D) The seventh
    (E) The eighth

15. If a large paperback book is at each end of the row and no clothbound book is next to a small paper-back book, which of the following must be true?

    (A) The second book is a small paperback book.
    (B) The fourth book is a clothbound book.
    (C) The sixth book is a leather-bound book.
    (D) The eighth book is a leather-bound book.
    (E) The tenth book is a clothbound book.

GO ON TO THE NEXT PAGE.

Questions 16-19

A plumber and an electrician have been hired to install the necessary plumbing and electrical fixtures in a new house. Each worker has four jobs, and each job takes exactly one day to complete. The workers will work together on four consecutive days, beginning on Monday. The work schedule for the plumber's jobs—G, H, I, and J—and for the electrician's jobs—L, M, N, and O—can be arranged at the convenience of each so long as the following conditions are met:

G and M cannot be done on the same day.
H and N must be done on the same day.
I must be done on the day immediately preceding the day on which G is done.
O must be done on a day preceding the day on which N is done.

16. Which of the following is an acceptable schedule for the plumber's jobs, beginning on Monday?

(A) G, H, J, I
(B) H, I, J, G
(C) H, J, G, I
(D) I, G, J, H
(E) J, H, G, I

17. Which of the following jobs CANNOT be scheduled for Monday?

(A) H
(B) I
(C) J
(D) L
(E) O

18. If H and N are scheduled for Wednesday, which of the following could be true?

(A) G is scheduled for Thursday.
(B) J is scheduled for Monday.
(C) L is scheduled for Monday.
(D) M is scheduled for Tuesday.
(E) O is scheduled for Thursday.

19. If J and M are scheduled for Thursday, which of the following must be true?

(A) G is scheduled for Monday.
(B) I is scheduled for Tuesday.
(C) L is scheduled for Wednesday.
(D) N is scheduled for Wednesday.
(E) O is scheduled for Monday.

Questions 20-22

A residential subdivision is accessible to vehicular traffic only as specified below:

All eight streets are one-way streets.
Access to the subdivision is at a single point F.
Exit from the subdivision is at a single point G.
The street intersections within the subdivision are W, X, Y, and Z.
Separate streets run directly

from F to W,
from W to X,
from W to Y,
from X to Z,
from X to W,
from Y to X,
from Z to Y, and
from Z to G.

20. Which of the following describes a possible route from F to G, including each of the intersections on that route?

(A) F − W − Z − G
(B) F − Y − X − G
(C) F − W − X − Y − G
(D) F − W − Y − X − G
(E) F − W − X − Z − G

21. For which of the following trips are there two alternative routes that do not have a street in common and do not go outside the subdivision?

(A) From W to Z
(B) From X to Y
(C) From X to Z
(D) From Y to W
(E) From Z to W

22. If, in traveling from F to G, a vehicle passes through no intersection more than once, which of the following could be, but need not be, a portion of that trip?

(A) From F to W
(B) From X to W
(C) From X to Z
(D) From Y to X
(E) From Z to Y

GO ON TO THE NEXT PAGE.

23. It was long thought that a now-rare disease of the joints, alkaptonuria, was epidemic in Egypt 2,500 years ago. Evidence came from the high proportion of mummies from that period showing symptoms of the disease. Recently, however, chemical analyses of skeletons have led scientists to propose that the joint damage was actually caused by chemicals used by Egyptian embalmers.

Which of the following, if true, would additionally weaken the traditional view that alkaptonuria afflicted many Egyptians 2,500 years ago?

(A) X-rays of the mummies showed shadows that clearly suggested joint damage, and recent inspection of the skeletons has confirmed that hypothesis.
(B) Although alkaptonuria is a disease that can be inherited, it did not appear in the descendants of the Egyptian population in which the symptoms were found.
(C) Egyptian embalming methods were highly secret, and scientists are still not certain of the nature of some of the chemicals that were used.
(D) Possible evidence of alkaptonuria has been pointed out in pictures representing the human figure found on artifacts left by other Middle Eastern cultures of that period.
(E) Some mummies of that period show no evidence of joint damage at all.

24. The Census Bureau reported that the median family income, after adjustment for inflation, increased 1.6 percent in 1983. Poverty normally declines when family income goes up, but the national poverty rate remained at its highest level in eighteen years in 1983. The Census Bureau offered two possible explanations: the lingering effects of the deep and lengthy 1981-1982 recession, and increases in the number of people living in families headed by women and in the number of adults not living with any relatives. Both groups are likely to be poorer than the population as a whole.

Which of the following conclusions can be properly drawn from this report?

(A) The national poverty rate has increased steadily over the last eighteen years.
(B) The national poverty rate will increase when there are lingering effects of an earlier recession.
(C) The median family income can increase even though the family income of some subgroups within the population declines or fails to increase.
(D) The category of adults not living with any relatives is the most critical group in the determination of whether the economy has improved.
(E) The median family income is affected more by changes in family patterns than by the extent of expansion or recession of the national economy.

GO ON TO THE NEXT PAGE.

25. For many people in the United States who are concerned about the cost of heating homes and businesses, wood has become an alternative energy source to coal, oil, and gas. Nevertheless, wood will never supply more than a modest fraction of our continuing energy needs.

Which of the following, if true, does NOT support the claim made in the last sentence in the passage above?

(A) There are many competing uses for a finite supply of wood, and suppliers give the lumber and paper industries a higher priority than they give individual consumers.
(B) Wood produces thick smoke in burning, and its extensive use in densely populated cities would violate federal antipollution guidelines.
(C) There are relatively narrow limits to how far wood can be trucked before it becomes more economical to burn the gasoline used for transportation instead of the wood.
(D) Most apartment dwellers do not have adequate storage space for the amount of wood necessary to supply energy for heating.
(E) Most commercial users of energy are located within range of a wood supply, and two-thirds of United States homes are located outside of metropolitan areas.

S T O P

IF YOU FINISH BEFORE TIME IS CALLED, YOU MAY CHECK YOUR WORK ON THIS SECTION ONLY.
DO NOT WORK ON ANY OTHER SECTION IN THE TEST.

SECTION 7

Time—30 minutes

25 Questions

Directions: Each question or group of questions is based on a passage or set of conditions. In answering some of the questions, it may be useful to draw a rough diagram. For each question, select the best answer choice given.

Questions 1-5

A florist has exactly seven varieties of flowers— P, Q, R, S, T, U, and V—from which she must select combinations of exactly five varieties with which to make flower arrangements. Any combination of the five varieties that conforms to all of the following conditions is acceptable:

If P is used in an arrangement, T cannot be used in that arrangement.
If Q is used in an arrangement, U must also be used in that arrangement.
If R is used in an arrangement, T must also be used in that arrangement.

1. Which of the following is an acceptable combination of varieties that the florist can select for an arrangement?

   (A) P, Q, S, T, U
   (B) P, Q, R, U, V
   (C) P, S, T, U, V
   (D) Q, R, S, U, V
   (E) Q, R, S, T, U

2. If the florist selects variety R to be included in an arrangement, which of the following must be true of that arrangement?

   (A) P is not used.
   (B) U is not used.
   (C) Q is used.
   (D) S is used.
   (E) V is used.

3. If variety P is used in an arrangement, which of the following CANNOT be used in that arrangement?

   (A) Q   (B) R   (C) S   (D) U   (E) V

4. If the florist does not select variety V for an arrangement, which of the following also CANNOT be selected?

   (A) P   (B) Q   (C) R   (D) S   (E) T

5. Which of the following substitutions can the florist always make without violating the conditions governing flower combination, provided the variety mentioned first was not, and the variety mentioned second was, originally going to be used in the arrangement concerned?

   (A) P for R
   (B) Q for U
   (C) R for T
   (D) S for V
   (E) V for T

GO ON TO THE NEXT PAGE.

6. Currently, the number of first-time admissions of individuals diagnosed as manic-depressives to hospitals in Great Britain exceeds by nine times the number of admissions of such patients to public and private hospitals in the United States, even though the population size of the United States is many times that of Great Britain.

Which of the following, if true, would be most useful to an attempt to explain the situation described above?

(A) The term manic-depressive refers to a wider range of mentally ill patients in Great Britain than it does in the United States.
(B) The admission rate in the United States includes those individuals who visit clinics for the first time as well as those who are admitted directly to hospitals.
(C) A small percentage of patients diagnosed as manic-depressive in Great Britain are admitted to private nursing homes rather than hospitals.
(D) The variety of training institutions in psychology in the United States is greater than in Great Britain, reflecting the variety of schools of psychology that have developed in the United States.
(E) Seeking professional assistance for mental health problems no longer carries a social stigma in the United States, as it once did.

7. Some soil scientists have asserted that decaying matter on the forest floor is a far greater source of the acidity in mountain lakes than is the acid rain that falls on these lakes. Therefore, they contend, reducing acid rain will not significantly reduce the acidity levels of mountain lakes.

Which of the following statements, if true, most seriously weakens the argument above?

(A) It is natural for mountain lakes to have acidity levels higher than those of other lakes.
(B) The harmful effects of increased acidity levels in lakes have been greatly underestimated.
(C) Acid rain is found in urban and heavily industrialized regions of the country.
(D) There is much disagreement among soil scientists about the causes of acid rain.
(E) While plant life remains, acid rain significantly increases the amount of decaying organic matter in natural environments.

8. Unlike other forms of narrative art, a play, to be successful, must give pleasure to its immediate audience by reflecting the concerns and values of that audience. A novel can achieve success over months or even years, but a play must be a hit or perish. Successful drama of the Restoration period, therefore, is a good index to the typical tastes and attitudes of its time.

The author of the passage above assumes that

(A) plays written for Restoration audiences do not appeal to modern audiences
(B) plays are superior to novels as a form of narrative art
(C) Restoration audiences were representative of the whole population of their time
(D) playgoers and novel readers are typically distinct and exclusive groups
(E) Restoration drama achieved popular success at the expense of critical success

GO ON TO THE NEXT PAGE.

Questions 9-13

A game has been invented that involves a player's directing a ball through four arches—1, 2, 3, and 4 in that order. On a certain day, the game is to be played on a circular lawn that has four major landmarks located around the border of the lawn at the points of the compass: to the north a lilac bush, to the east an oak tree, to the south a rock garden, and to the west a small pond. The arches can be placed on the lawn in any numerical arrangement as long as the following conditions are met:

The four arches must be positioned at equal distances around the border of the lawn, and each arch must stand on the border midway between two adjacent landmarks.

The lilac bush must be one of the landmarks that stand nearest to arch 1.

The rock garden must be one of the landmarks that stand nearest to arch 2.

The pond must be one of the landmarks that stand nearest to arch 4.

The pond cannot be one of the landmarks that stand nearest to arch 1.

9. Which of the following is a possible arrangement of the four arches as they are positioned in relation to the four landmarks?

(A) Lilac bush -1- oak tree -3- rock garden -4- pond -2- lilac bush
(B) Lilac bush -1- oak tree -3- rock garden -2- pond -4- lilac bush
(C) Lilac bush -1- oak tree -4- rock garden -2- pond -3- lilac bush
(D) Lilac bush -3- oak tree -2- rock garden -4- pond -1- lilac bush
(E) Lilac bush -3- oak tree -1- rock garden -2- pond -4- lilac bush

10. Which of the arches can be placed directly between the rock garden and the pond?

(A) 2 but not 1, 3, or 4
(B) 3 but not 1, 2, or 4
(C) 2 or 3 but not 1 or 4
(D) 2 or 4 but not 1 or 3
(E) 2, 3, or 4 but not 1

11. If arch 3 is one of the arches nearest to the rock garden, which of the following must be true?

(A) Arch 2 is one of the arches nearest to the oak tree.
(B) Arch 2 is one of the arches nearest to the pond.
(C) Arch 3 is one of the arches nearest to the oak tree.
(D) Arch 4 is one of the arches nearest to the lilac bush.
(E) Arch 4 is one of the arches nearest to the rock garden.

12. If arch 3 is separated from arch 4 by exactly one landmark, any of the following can be true EXCEPT:

(A) Arch 2 is one of the arches nearest to the pond.
(B) Arch 3 is one of the arches nearest to the rock garden.
(C) Arch 3 is one of the arches nearest to the pond.
(D) Arch 4 is one of the arches nearest to the lilac bush.
(E) Arch 4 is one of the arches nearest to the rock garden.

13. Which of the following placements of one of the arches allows more than one possible arrangement of the arches on the lawn?

(A) Arch 2 between the rock garden and the pond
(B) Arch 3 between the lilac bush and the pond
(C) Arch 3 between the rock garden and the pond
(D) Arch 4 between the rock garden and the pond
(E) Arch 4 between the lilac bush and the pond

GO ON TO THE NEXT PAGE.

Questions 14-18

P, Q, R, S, T are the computers in the five overseas offices of a large multinational corporation. The computers are linked in an unusual manner in order to provide increased security for the data in certain offices. Data can be directly requested only from:

P by Q
P by T
Q by P
R by P
S by Q
S by T
T by R

If a computer can directly request data from another computer, then it can also pass on requests for data to that other computer.

14. Which of the following computers CANNOT request data from any of the other four computers?

(A) P   (B) Q   (C) R   (D) S   (E) T

15. Which of the following is a complete and accurate list of computers that can request data from S through exactly one other computer?

(A) P and Q
(B) P and R
(C) Q and R
(D) R and T
(E) P, Q, and T

16. Which of the following requests for data requires the greatest number of intervening requests for data?

(A) A request by P for data from Q
(B) A request by Q for data from R
(C) A request by Q for data from T
(D) A request by R for data from P
(E) A request by R for data from S

17. If computers Q, R, S, and T are the only ones operating, which of the following requests for data can be made, either directly or through one or more of the other computers?

(A) A request by Q for data from T
(B) A request by T for data from R
(C) A request by S for data from Q
(D) A request by R for data from Q
(E) A request by R for data from S

18. If computers P, R, S, and T are the only ones operating, which of the following requests for data can be made NEITHER directly NOR through exactly one of the other operating computers?

(A) A request by P for data from S
(B) A request by P for data from T
(C) A request by P for data from R
(D) A request by R for data from S
(E) A request by T for data from S

GO ON TO THE NEXT PAGE.

Questions 19-22

A map is being prepared that will represent the following seven provinces of a certain country: Gusaya, Istoria, Jacaranda, Luna, Praz, Serenia, and Venotia.

Gusaya has common borders with all of the other six provinces on the map except Jacaranda.

Istoria has common borders with exactly four other provinces—Gusaya, Jacaranda, Praz, and Venotia.

Jacaranda has common borders with exactly two other provinces—Istoria and Praz.

Luna has common borders with exactly two other provinces—Gusaya and Venotia.

Praz has common borders with exactly three other provinces—Gusaya, Istoria, and Jacaranda.

Serenia has a common border only with Gusaya.

Venotia has common borders with exactly three other provinces—Gusaya, Istoria, and Luna.

Exactly six colors—gold, jade, olive, red, silver, and white—will be used in representing the seven provinces. Each color will be used at least once. Each province will be one solid color on the map. The following restrictions apply to the map's colors:

No province can be the same color as any province bordering on it.

Jade and olive cannot be used for provinces bordering on each other.

Silver and white cannot be used for provinces bordering on each other.

Gusaya must be red.

Istoria must be jade.

19. Which of the following provinces can NEITHER be red NOR be jade on this map?

(A) Istoria
(B) Jacaranda
(C) Luna
(D) Praz
(E) Serenia

20. Which of the following provinces could be olive on this map?

(A) Gusaya
(B) Jacaranda
(C) Praz
(D) Serenia
(E) Venotia

21. If Venotia and Jacaranda are white on the map, Serenia must be

(A) gold
(B) jade
(C) olive
(D) silver
(E) white

22. If Serenia is gold, which of the following provinces must be olive?

(A) Istoria
(B) Jacaranda
(C) Luna
(D) Praz
(E) Venotia

GO ON TO THE NEXT PAGE.

23. It is important to teach students to use computers effectively. Therefore, students should be taught computer programming in school.

Which of the following, if true, most weakens the argument above?

(A) Only people who use computers effectively are skilled at computer programming.
(B) Only people skilled at computer programming use computers effectively.
(C) Some people who use computers effectively cannot write computer programs.
(D) Some schools teach computer programming more effectively than others.
(E) Most people who are able to program computers use computers effectively.

24. Butterfat gets its yellowish color from carotene, the fat-soluble vitamin A precursor that is also responsible for the color of carrots. Not all butterfat, however, is equally yellow. Some breeds of cows are more efficient than others at converting carotene to the colorless vitamin A.

If butter made from the milk of holstein cows is much paler than that made from the milk of jersey or guernsey cows, then the facts above suggest that

(A) there is less butterfat in the milk of holsteins than in the milk of jerseys or guernseys
(B) there is more vitamin A in the butterfat of holsteins than in the butterfat of jerseys or guernseys
(C) there is more carotene in the butterfat of holsteins than in the butterfat of jerseys or guernseys
(D) holsteins are less efficient converters of carotene than are jerseys or guernseys
(E) the carotene in the milk of holsteins is less fat-soluble than the carotene in the milk of jerseys or guernseys

25. X melts at a higher temperature than P melts.
Y melts at a lower temperature than P melts, but at a higher temperature than Q melts.

If the statements above are true, it can be concluded with certainty that S melts at a higher temperature than Y melts if one knows in addition that

(A) Q and P melt at a higher temperature than S melts
(B) X melts at a higher temperature than S melts
(C) P melts at a lower temperature than S melts
(D) Q melts at the same temperature that S melts
(E) S melts at a higher temperature than Q melts

S T O P

IF YOU FINISH BEFORE TIME IS CALLED, YOU MAY CHECK YOUR WORK ON THIS SECTION ONLY.
DO NOT WORK ON ANY OTHER SECTION IN THE TEST.

THE GRADUATE RECORD EXAMINATIONS
GENERAL TEST

You will have 3 hours and 30 minutes in which to work on this test, which consists of seven sections. During the time allowed for one section, you may work only on that section. The time allowed for each section is 30 minutes.

Your score will be based on the number of questions for which you select the best answer choice given. No deduction will be made for a question for which you do not select the best answer choice given. Therefore, you are advised to answer all questions.

You are advised to work as rapidly as you can without losing accuracy. Do not spend too much time on questions that are too difficult for you. Go on to the other questions and come back to the difficult ones later.

There are several different types of questions; you will find special directions for each type in the test itself. Be sure you understand the directions before attempting to answer any questions.

For each question several answer choices (lettered A-E or A-D) are given from which you are to select the ONE best answer. YOU MUST INDICATE ALL OF YOUR ANSWERS ON THE SEPARATE ANSWER SHEET. No credit will be given for anything written in this examination book, but to work out your answers you may write in the book as much as you wish. After you have decided which of the suggested answers is best, blacken the corresponding space on the answer sheet. Be sure to:

- Use a soft black lead pencil (No. 2 or HB).

- Mark only one answer to each question. No credit will be given for multiple answers.

- Mark your answer in the row with the same number as the number of the question you are answering.

- Carefully and completely blacken the space corresponding to the answer you select for each question. Fill the space with a dark mark so that you cannot see the letter inside the space. Light or partial marks may not be read by the scoring machine. See the example of proper and improper answer marks below.

- Erase all stray marks. If you change an answer, be sure that you completely erase the old answer before marking your new answer. Incomplete erasures may be read as intended answers.

Example: Sample Answer

What city is the capital of France?   (A) ● (C) (D) (E)   BEST ANSWER
                                                                        PROPERLY MARKED

(A) Rome   (A) (B) (C) (D) (E)
(B) Paris   (A) (B) (C) (D) (E)
(C) London   (A) (B) (C) (D) (E)   IMPROPER MARKS
(D) Cairo   (A) (B) (C) (D) (E)
(E) Oslo   (A) (B) (C) (D) (E)

Do not be concerned that the answer sheet provides spaces for more answers than there are questions in the test. Some or all of the passages for this test have been adapted from published material to provide the examinee with significant problems for analysis and evaluation. To make the passages suitable for testing purposes, the style, content, or point of view of the original may have been altered in some cases. The ideas contained in the passages do not necessarily represent the opinions of the Graduate Record Examinations Board or Educational Testing Service.

CLOSE YOUR TEST BOOK AND WAIT FOR FURTHER INSTRUCTIONS FROM THE SUPERVISOR.

I

NOTE: To ensure the prompt and accurate processing of test results, your cooperation in following these directions is needed. The procedures that follow have been kept to the minimum necessary. They will take a few minutes to complete, but it is essential that you fill in all blanks <u>exactly</u> as directed.

GENERAL TEST

A. Print and sign your full name in this box:

PRINT: _____

         (LAST)   (FIRST)   (MIDDLE)

SIGN: _____

B. Your answer sheet contains areas which will be used to ensure accurate reporting of your test results. It is essential that you fill in these areas <u>exactly</u> as explained below.

[1] YOUR NAME, MAILING ADDRESS, AND TEST CENTER: Place your answer sheet so that the heading "Graduate Record Examinations—General Test" is at the top. In box 1 below that heading <u>print</u> your name. Enter your current mailing address. Print the name of the city, state or province, and country in which the test center is located, and the center number.

[2] YOUR NAME: <u>Print</u> all the information requested in the boxes at the top of the columns (first four letters of your last name, your first initial, and middle initial), and then fill in completely the appropriate space beneath each entry.

[3] DATE OF BIRTH: Fill in completely the space beside the month in which you were born. Then enter the day of the month on which you were born in the boxes at the top of the columns. Fill in completely the appropriate space beneath each entry. Be sure to treat zeros like any other digit, and to add a zero before any single digit; for example 03, not 3. (Your year of birth is not required on the answer sheet.)

[4] SEX: Fill in completely the appropriate space.

[5] REGISTRATION NUMBER: Copy your registration number from your admission ticket into the boxes at the top of the columns and then fill in completely the appropriate space beneath each entry. Check your admission ticket again to make certain that you have copied your registration number accurately.

[6] TITLE CODE: Copy the numbers shown below and fill in completely the appropriate spaces beneath each entry as shown. When you have completed item 6, check to be sure it is identical to the illustration below.

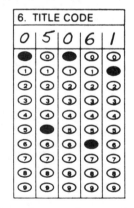

[7] CERTIFICATION STATEMENT: In the boxed area, please write (do not print) the following statement: I certify that I am the person whose name appears on this answer sheet. I also agree not to disclose the contents of the test I am taking today to anyone. Sign and date where indicated.

[8] FORM CODE: Copy _GR87-5_ in the box.

[9] TEST BOOK SERIAL NUMBER: Copy the serial number of your test book in the box. It is printed in red at the upper right on the front cover of your test book.

C. WHEN YOU HAVE FINISHED THESE INSTRUCTIONS, PLEASE TURN YOUR ANSWER SHEET OVER AND SIGN YOUR NAME IN THE BOX EXACTLY AS YOU DID FOR ITEM [7].

When you have finished, wait for further instructions from the supervisor. DO NOT OPEN YOUR TEST BOOK UNTIL YOU ARE TOLD TO DO SO.

FOR GENERAL TEST, FORM GR87-5 ONLY
Answer Key and Percentages* of Examinees Answering Each Question Correctly

VERBAL ABILITY						QUANTITATIVE ABILITY						ANALYTICAL ABILITY					
Section 1			Section 2			Section 3			Section 4			Section 5			Section 7		
Number	Answer	P+	Number	Answer	P+	Number	Answer	P+	Number	Answer	P+	Number	Answer	P+	Number	Answer	P+
1	C	83	1	C	91	1	A	95	1	B	90	1	A	71	1	E	87
2	A	80	2	D	56	2	C	92	2	C	89	2	A	64	2	A	91
3	C	57	3	D	66	3	B	84	3	C	89	3	B	53	3	B	94
4	B	59	4	A	72	4	B	83	4	D	85	4	C	71	4	A	70
5	E	51	5	B	63	5	D	81	5	A	82	5	A	69	5	D	70
6	C	47	6	B	46	6	A	76	6	B	82	6	C	66	6	A	81
7	C	21	7	B	48	7	A	74	7	C	82	7	E	91	7	E	51
8	C	92	8	B	88	8	A	81	8	B	80	8	D	63	8	C	69
9	A	86	9	C	89	9	B	69	9	C	69	9	B	74	9	B	67
10	E	82	10	D	88	10	D	59	10	A	68	10	D	50	10	E	38
11	B	77	11	A	68	11	C	60	11	A	58	11	E	35	11	D	30
12	A	45	12	C	55	12	A	49	12	B	65	12	B	56	12	A	33
13	D	55	13	E	39	13	C	49	13	D	59	13	E	41	13	E	32
14	E	21	14	D	37	14	C	41	14	A	42	14	A	46	14	D	70
15	E	17	15	B	22	15	D	31	15	D	49	15	C	37	15	B	46
16	A	9	16	A	27	16	A	95	16	A	95	16	D	53	16	C	41
17	D	79	17	A	44	17	D	90	17	E	77	17	A	40	17	E	36
18	D	43	18	C	51	18	D	80	18	B	74	18	C	33	18	A	42
19	B	58	19	E	25	19	E	81	19	D	72	19	D	21	19	D	27
20	C	36	20	B	38	20	E	53	20	C	59	20	E	27	20	D	39
21	E	64	21	D	64	21	B	83	21	B	91	21	B	33	21	D	26
22	B	53	22	B	69	22	A	76	22	B	81	22	D	19	22	C	37
23	A	59	23	C	72	23	E	49	23	D	55	23	B	51	23	C	55
24	C	58	24	A	40	24	D	47	24	C	58	24	C	49	24	B	41
25	B	70	25	B	42	25	D	48	25	C	46	25	E	44	25	C	50
26	C	63	26	E	49	26	C	45	26	B	61						
27	D	76	27	A	58	27	B	51	27	C	57						
28	A	94	28	A	91	28	C	47	28	D	29						
29	C	71	29	A	86	29	A	36	29	A	34						
30	A	66	30	D	83	30	A	25	30	E	36						
31	A	60	31	D	73												
32	D	43	32	A	73												
33	A	45	33	E	46												
34	B	45	34	B	50												
35	D	39	35	E	25												
36	A	37	36	E	31												
37	E	38	37	C	25												
38	E	27	38	D	20												

*Estimated P+ for the group of examinees who took the GRE General Test in a recent three-year period.

SCORE CONVERSIONS AND PERCENTS BELOW* for GRE GENERAL TEST, FORM GR87-5 ONLY

Raw Score	Verbal Score	% Below	Quantitative Score	% Below	Analytical Score	% Below	Raw Score	Verbal Score	% Below	Quantitative Score	% Below	Analytical Score	% Below
73-76	800	99					40	450	43	550	49	720	93
72	790	99					39	440	40	540	46	710	92
71	780	99					38	430	37	530	44	690	89
							37	430	37	520	42	680	88
70	760	99					36	420	34	510	39	670	86
69	750	98											
68	740	98					35	410	31	490	34	650	84
67	730	97					34	400	28	480	32	640	81
66	720	96					33	390	26	470	30	630	78
							32	390	26	460	27	610	74
65	700	95					31	380	24	450	26	600	72
64	690	94											
63	680	93					30	370	22	430	21	590	69
62	670	92					29	360	18	420	19	570	64
61	660	91					28	350	17	410	18	560	61
							27	350	17	400	16	540	56
60	650	89	800	98			26	340	15	390	14	530	53
59	640	88	780	97									
58	630	86	770	95			25	330	13	370	11	520	50
57	610	84	760	94			24	320	11	360	10	500	44
56	600	82	750	92			23	310	10	350	9	490	41
							22	300	8	340	8	470	36
55	590	80	730	89			21	300	8	320	6	460	33
54	580	78	720	87									
53	570	75	710	85			20	290	7	310	5	440	27
52	560	73	700	83			19	280	6	300	4	420	23
51	550	71	690	81			18	270	4	290	3	410	21
							17	260	3	280	3	390	16
50	540	68	670	77	800	99	16	250	3	260	2	370	13
49	530	65	660	74	800	99							
48	530	65	650	72	800	99	15	240	2	250	1	360	11
47	520	63	640	71	800	99	14	230	1	240	1	340	9
46	510	60	630	68	790	98	13	220	1	230	1	310	5
							12	210	1	220	1	290	3
45	500	57	610	63	780	98	11	200	0	200	0	270	2
44	490	55	600	61	770	98							
43	480	52	590	59	760	97	10	200	0	200	0	250	1
42	470	49	580	56	740	95	9	200	0	200	0	240	1
41	460	45	570	53	730	94	8	200	0	200	0	220	1
							0-7	200	0	200	0	200	0

*Percent scoring below the scaled score, based on the performance of the 816,621 examinees who took the General Test between October 1, 1983, and September 30, 1986.

01

THE GRADUATE RECORD
EXAMINATIONS

General Test

SECTION 1
Time—30 minutes
38 Questions

Directions: Each sentence below has one or two blanks, each blank indicating that something has been omitted. Beneath the sentence are five lettered words or sets of words. Choose the word or set of words for each blank that best fits the meaning of the sentence as a whole.

1. By divesting himself of all regalities, the former king ------- the consideration that customarily protects monarchs.

    (A) merited   (B) forfeited   (C) debased
    (D) concealed   (E) extended

2. A perennial goal in zoology is to infer function from -------, relating the ------- of an organism to its physical form and cellular organization.

    (A) age..ancestry
    (B) classification..appearance
    (C) size..movement
    (D) structure..behavior
    (E) location..habitat

3. The sociologist responded to the charge that her new theory was ------- by pointing out that it did not in fact contradict accepted sociological principles.

    (A) banal   (B) heretical   (C) unproven
    (D) complex   (E) superficial

4. Industrialists seized economic power only after industry had ------- agriculture as the preeminent form of production; previously such power had ------- land ownership.

    (A) sabotaged..threatened
    (B) overtaken..produced
    (C) toppled..culminated in
    (D) joined..relied on
    (E) supplanted..resided in

5. Rumors, embroidered with detail, live on for years, neither denied nor confirmed, until they become accepted as fact even among people not known for their -------.

    (A) insight   (B) obstinacy   (C) introspection
    (D) tolerance   (E) credulity

6. No longer ------- by the belief that the world around us was expressly designed for humanity, many people try to find intellectual ------- for that lost certainty in astrology and in mysticism.

    (A) satisfied..reasons
    (B) sustained..substitutes
    (C) reassured..justifications
    (D) hampered..equivalents
    (E) restricted..parallels

7. People should not be praised for their virtue if they lack the energy to be -------; in such cases, goodness is merely the effect of -------.

    (A) depraved..hesitation
    (B) cruel..effortlessness
    (C) wicked..indolence
    (D) unjust..boredom
    (E) iniquitous..impiety

GO ON TO THE NEXT PAGE.

Directions: In each of the following questions, a related pair of words or phrases is followed by five lettered pairs of words or phrases. Select the lettered pair that best expresses a relationship similar to that expressed in the original pair.

8. SKELETON : ANIMAL :: (A) ivory : piano
   (B) peel : fruit   (C) ore : mine
    (D) mast : ship   (E) framing : building

9. OUTSKIRTS : TOWN ::
   (A) rung : ladder
   (B) trunk : tree
   (C) water : goblet
   (D) margin : page
   (E) hangar : airplane

10. AMORPHOUSNESS : DEFINITION ::
    (A) lassitude : energy
    (B) spontaneity : awareness
    (C) angularity : intricacy
    (D) rectitude : drabness
    (E) precision : uniformity

11. COLLUSION : CONSPIRATORS ::
    (A) conclusion : messengers
    (B) revision : correspondents
    (C) identification : arbitrators
    (D) attribution : interpreters
    (E) cooperation : partners

12. DIVERT : SHUNT :: (A) file : collate
    (B) collide : dent   (C) guess : calibrate
     (D) retard : brake   (E) inspect : magnify

13. EQUIVOCATE : COMMITMENT ::
    (A) procrastinate : action
    (B) implicate : exposition
    (C) expostulate : confusion
    (D) corroborate : falsification
    (E) fabricate : explanation

14. ARMADA : VEHICLES ::
    (A) drill : recruits
    (B) planning : logistics
    (C) infantry : cavalry
    (D) fusillade : projectiles
    (E) supply : munitions

15. LACONIC : SPEECH ::
    (A) believable : excuse
    (B) unyielding : attitude
    (C) austere : design
    (D) somber : procession
    (E) gradual : transition

16. GROW : BURGEON :: (A) beat : palpitate
    (B) transport : enrapture   (C) flourish : thrive
     (D) rot : decay   (E) evolve : multiply

GO ON TO THE NEXT PAGE.

<u>Directions:</u> Each passage in this group is followed by questions based on its content. After reading a passage, choose the best answer to each question. Answer all questions following a passage on the basis of what is <u>stated</u> or <u>implied</u> in that passage.

The belief that art originates in intuitive rather than rational faculties was worked out historically and philosophically in the somewhat wearisome volumes of Benedetto Croce, who is usually considered the originator of a new aesthetic. Croce was, in fact, expressing a very old idea. Long before the Romantics stressed intuition and self-expression, the frenzy of inspiration was regarded as fundamental to art, but philosophers had always assumed it must be controlled by law and by the intellectual power of putting things into harmonious order. This general philosophic concept of art was supported by technical necessities. It was necessary to master certain laws and to use intellect in order to build Gothic cathedrals, or set up the stained glass windows of Chartres. When this bracing element of craftsmanship ceased to dominate artists' outlook, new technical elements had to be adopted to maintain the intellectual element in art. Such were linear perspective and anatomy.

17. The passage suggests that which of the following would most likely have occurred if linear perspective and anatomy had not come to influence artistic endeavor?

(A) The craftsmanship that shaped Gothic architecture would have continued to dominate artists' outlooks.

(B) Some other technical elements would have been adopted to discipline artistic inspiration.

(C) Intellectual control over artistic inspiration would not have influenced painting as it did architecture.

(D) The role of intuitive inspiration would not have remained fundamental to theories of artistic creation.

(E) The assumptions of aesthetic philosophers before Croce would have been invalidated.

18. The passage supplies information for answering which of the following questions?

(A) Does Romantic art exhibit the triumph of intuition over intellect?

(B) Did an emphasis on linear perspective and anatomy dominate Romantic art?

(C) Are the intellectual and intuitive faculties harmoniously balanced in post-Romantic art?

(D) Are the effects of the rational control of artistic inspiration evident in the great works of pre-Romantic eras?

(E) Was the artistic craftsmanship displayed in Gothic cathedrals also an element in paintings of this period?

19. The passage implies that which of the following was a traditional assumption of aesthetic philosophers?

(A) Intellectual elements in art exert a necessary control over artistic inspiration.

(B) Architecture has never again reached the artistic greatness of the Gothic cathedrals.

(C) Aesthetic philosophy is determined by the technical necessities of art.

(D) Artistic craftsmanship is more important in architectural art than in pictorial art.

(E) Paintings lacked the intellectual element before the invention of linear perspective and anatomy.

20. The author mentions "linear perspective and anatomy" in the last sentence in order to do which of the following?

(A) Expand his argument to include painting as well as architecture

(B) Indicate his disagreement with Croce's theory of the origins of art

(C) Support his point that rational order of some kind has often seemed to discipline artistic inspiration

(D) Explain the rational elements in Gothic painting that corresponded to craftsmanship in Gothic architecture

(E) Show the increasing sophistication of artists after the Gothic period

GO ON TO THE NEXT PAGE.

(The passage below is drawn from an article published in 1962.)

Computer programmers often remark that computing machines, with a perfect lack of discrimination, will do any foolish thing they are told to do. The reason for this lies, of course, in the narrow fixation of the computing machine's "intelligence" on the details of its own perceptions—its inability to be guided by any large context. In a psychological description of the computer intelligence, three related adjectives come to mind: single-minded, literal-minded, and simpleminded. Recognizing this, we should at the same time recognize that this single-mindedness, literal-mindedness, and simplemindedness also characterizes theoretical mathematics, though to a lesser extent.

Since science tries to deal with reality, even the most precise sciences normally work with more or less imperfectly understood approximations toward which scientists must maintain an appropriate skepticism. Thus, for instance, it may come as a shock to mathematicians to learn that the Schrödinger equation for the hydrogen atom is not a literally correct description of this atom, but only an approximation to a somewhat more correct equation taking account of spin, magnetic dipole, and relativistic effects; and that this corrected equation is itself only an imperfect approximation to an infinite set of quantum field-theoretical equations. Physicists, looking at the original Schrödinger equation, learn to sense in it the presence of many invisible terms in addition to the differential terms visible, and this sense inspires an entirely appropriate disregard for the purely technical features of the equation. This very healthy skepticism is foreign to the mathematical approach.

Mathematics must deal with well-defined situations. Thus, mathematicians depend on an intellectual effort outside of mathematics for the crucial specification of the approximation that mathematics is to take literally. Give mathematicians a situation that is the least bit ill-defined, and they will make it well-defined, perhaps appropriately, but perhaps inappropriately. In some cases, the mathematicians' literal-mindedness may have unfortunate consequences. The mathematicians turn the scientists' theoretical assumptions, that is, their convenient points of analytical emphasis, into axioms, and then take these axioms literally. This brings the danger that they may also persuade the scientists to take these axioms literally. The question, central to the scientific investigation but intensely disturbing in the mathematical context—what happens if the axioms are relaxed?—is thereby ignored.

The physicist rightly dreads precise argument, since an argument that is convincing only if it is precise loses all its force if the assumptions on which it is based are slightly changed, whereas an argument that is convincing though imprecise may well be stable under small perturbations of its underlying assumptions.

21. The author discusses computing machines in the first paragraph primarily in order to do which of the following?

(A) Indicate the dangers inherent in relying to a great extent on machines
(B) Illustrate his views about the approach of mathematicians to problem solving
(C) Compare the work of mathematicians with that of computer programmers
(D) Provide one definition of intelligence
(E) Emphasize the importance of computers in modern technological society

22. According to the passage, scientists are skeptical toward their equations because scientists

(A) work to explain real, rather than theoretical or simplified, situations
(B) know that well-defined problems are often the most difficult to solve
(C) are unable to express their data in terms of multiple variables
(D) are unwilling to relax the axioms they have developed
(E) are unable to accept mathematical explanations of natural phenomena

23. It can be inferred from the passage that scientists make which of the following assumptions about scientific arguments?

(A) The literal truth of the arguments can be made clear only in a mathematical context.
(B) The arguments necessarily ignore the central question of scientific investigation.
(C) The arguments probably will be convincing only to other scientists.
(D) The conclusions of the arguments do not necessarily follow from their premises.
(E) The premises on which the arguments are based may change.

GO ON TO THE NEXT PAGE.

24. According to the passage, mathematicians present a danger to scientists for which of the following reasons?

    (A) Mathematicians may provide theories that are incompatible with those already developed by scientists.
    (B) Mathematicians may define situations in a way that is incomprehensible to scientists.
    (C) Mathematicians may convince scientists that theoretical assumptions are facts.
    (D) Scientists may come to believe that axiomatic statements are untrue.
    (E) Scientists may begin to provide arguments that are convincing but imprecise.

25. The author suggests that the approach of physicists to solving scientific problems is which of the following?

    (A) Practical for scientific purposes
    (B) Detrimental to scientific progress
    (C) Unimportant in most situations
    (D) Expedient, but of little long-term value
    (E) Effective, but rarely recognized as such

26. The author suggests that a mathematician asked to solve a problem in an ill-defined situation would first attempt to do which of the following?

    (A) Identify an analogous situation
    (B) Simplify and define the situation
    (C) Vary the underlying assumptions of a description of the situation
    (D) Determine what use would be made of the solution provided
    (E) Evaluate the theoretical assumptions that might explain the situation

27. The author implies that scientists develop a healthy skepticism because they are aware that

    (A) mathematicians are better able to solve problems than are scientists
    (B) changes in axiomatic propositions will inevitably undermine scientific arguments
    (C) well-defined situations are necessary for the design of reliable experiments
    (D) mathematical solutions can rarely be applied to real problems
    (E) some factors in most situations must remain unknown

GO ON TO THE NEXT PAGE.

Directions: Each question below consists of a word printed in capital letters, followed by five lettered words or phrases. Choose the lettered word or phrase that is most nearly <u>opposite</u> in meaning to the word in capital letters.

Since some of the questions require you to distinguish fine shades of meaning, be sure to consider all the choices before deciding which one is best.

28. EVACUATE: (A) boil off   (B) fill up
(C) melt down   (D) neutralize   (E) spin

29. OUTLANDISH: (A) prolific
(B) unchanging   (C) conventional
(D) noticeable   (E) transparent

30. INHIBITOR: (A) catalyst   (B) acid
(C) solution   (D) reaction   (E) compound

31. CONSTRICT: (A) expiate   (B) deviate
(C) dilate   (D) accelerate   (E) vindicate

32. REPORTORIAL: (A) unlikely
(B) imaginative   (C) indecisive
(D) characteristic   (E) challenging

33. INDIGENCE: (A) wealth   (B) vanity
(C) boldness   (D) endurance   (E) vivacity

34. INVEIGLE:
(A) display openly   (B) request directly
(C) initiate willingly   (D) advocate strongly
(E) contribute lavishly

35. TRACTABLE: (A) distraught   (B) irritating
(C) ruthless   (D) headstrong   (E) lazy

36. INCHOATE:
(A) sensuously pleasant
(B) prominently visible
(C) intrinsically reasonable
(D) fully formed
(E) widely known

37. PERFIDY: (A) thoroughness   (B) generosity
(C) gratitude   (D) tact   (E) loyalty

38. APPROPRIATE: (A) create a void
(B) rectify an error   (C) sanction
(D) surrender   (E) lend

S T O P

IF YOU FINISH BEFORE TIME IS CALLED, YOU MAY CHECK YOUR WORK ON THIS SECTION ONLY.
DO NOT WORK ON ANY OTHER SECTION IN THE TEST.

Section 2 starts on page 124.

SECTION 2
Time—30 minutes
38 Questions

Directions: Each sentence below has one or two blanks, each blank indicating that something has been omitted. Beneath the sentence are five lettered words or sets of words. Choose the word or set of words for each blank that best fits the meaning of the sentence as a whole.

1. Animals that have tasted unpalatable plants tend to ------- them afterward on the basis of their most conspicuous features, such as their flowers.

   (A) recognize   (B) hoard   (C) trample
   (D) retrieve   (E) approach

2. As for the alleged value of expert opinion, one need only ------- government records to see ------- evidence of the failure of such opinions in many fields.

   (A) inspect. .questionable
   (B) retain. .circumstantial
   (C) distribute. .possible
   (D) consult. .strong
   (E) evaluate. .problematic

3. In scientific inquiry it becomes a matter of duty to expose a ------- hypothesis to every possible kind of -------.

   (A) tentative. .examination
   (B) debatable. .approximation
   (C) well-established. .rationalization
   (D) logical. .elaboration
   (E) suspect. .correlation

4. Charlotte Salomon's biography is a reminder that the currents of private life, however diverted, dislodged, or twisted by ------- public events, retain their hold on the ------- recording them.

   (A) transitory. .culture
   (B) dramatic. .majority
   (C) overpowering. .individual
   (D) conventional. .audience
   (E) relentless. .institution

5. Philosophical problems arise when people ask questions that, though very -------, have certain characteristics in common.

   (A) relevant
   (B) elementary
   (C) abstract
   (D) diverse
   (E) controversial

6. Although Johnson ------- great enthusiasm for his employees' project, in reality his interest in the project was so ------- as to be almost non-existent.

   (A) generated. .redundant
   (B) displayed. .preemptive
   (C) expected. .indiscriminate
   (D) feigned. .perfunctory
   (E) demanded. .dispassionate

7. Not all the indicators necessary to convey the effect of depth in a picture work simultaneously; the picture's illusion of ------- three-dimensional appearance must therefore result from the viewer's integration of various indicators perceived -------.

   (A) imitative. .coincidentally
   (B) uniform. .successively
   (C) temporary. .comprehensively
   (D) expressive. .sympathetically
   (E) schematic. .passively

GO ON TO THE NEXT PAGE.

Directions: In each of the following questions, a related pair of words or phrases is followed by five lettered pairs of words or phrases. Select the lettered pair that best expresses a relationship similar to that expressed in the original pair.

8. GADGETS : TOOLS :: (A) blankets : linen
   (B) leaflets : posters   (C) trinkets : jewelry
    (D) sockets : bulbs   (E) ringlets : hair

9. LISTEN : RECORDING :: (A) carve : statue
   (B) reproduce : plan   (C) review : book
    (D) frame : painting   (E) view : photograph

10. CENSORSHIP : INFORMATION ::
    (A) frugality : constraint
    (B) sampling : measurement
    (C) sanitation : disease
    (D) cultivation : erosion
    (E) philanthropy : generosity

11. DELUGE : DROPLET ::
    (A) beach : wave
    (B) desert : oasis
    (C) blizzard : icicle
    (D) landslide : pebble
    (E) cloudburst : puddle

12. SPEAK : RETICENT ::
    (A) spend : parsimonious
    (B) excel : audacious
    (C) commend : irate
    (D) work : servile
    (E) invent : diffident

13. PATRIOTIC : CHAUVINISTIC ::
    (A) impudent : intolerant
    (B) furtive : surreptitious
    (C) incisive : trenchant
    (D) receptive : gullible
    (E) verbose : prolix

14. BOUQUET : FLOWERS :: (A) forest : trees
    (B) husk : corn   (C) mist : rain
     (D) woodpile : logs   (E) drift : snow

15. ENDEMIC : REGION ::
    (A) homogeneous : population
    (B) inborn : individual
    (C) hybrid : species
    (D) sporadic : time
    (E) aberrant : norm

16. PECCADILLO : SIN ::
    (A) provocation : instigation
    (B) anxiety : fear
    (C) perjury : corruption
    (D) penury : poverty
    (E) admonishment : castigation

GO ON TO THE NEXT PAGE.

Directions: Each passage in this group is followed by questions based on its content. After reading a passage, choose the best answer to each question. Answer all questions following a passage on the basis of what is stated or implied in that passage.

In eighteenth-century France and England, reformers rallied around egalitarian ideals, but few reformers advocated higher education for women. Although the public decried women's lack of education, it did not encourage learning for its own sake for women. In spite of the general prejudice against learned women, there was one place where women could exhibit their erudition: the literary salon. Many writers have defined the woman's role in the salon as that of an intelligent hostess, but the salon had more than a social function for women. It was an informal university, too, where women exchanged ideas with educated persons, read their own works and heard those of others, and received and gave criticism.

In the 1750's, when salons were firmly established in France, some English women, who called themselves "Bluestockings," followed the example of the *salonnières* (French salon hostesses) and formed their own salons. Most Bluestockings did not wish to mirror the *salonnières*; they simply desired to adapt a proven formula to their own purpose—the elevation of women's status through moral and intellectual training. Differences in social orientation and background can account perhaps for differences in the nature of French and English salons. The French salon incorporated aristocratic attitudes that exalted courtly pleasure and emphasized artistic accomplishments. The English Bluestockings, originating from a more modest background, emphasized learning and work over pleasure. Accustomed to the regimented life of court circles, *salonnières* tended toward formality in their salons. The English women, though somewhat puritanical, were more casual in their approach.

At first, the Bluestockings did imitate the *salonnières* by including men in their circles. However, as they gained cohesion, the Bluestockings came to regard themselves as a women's group and to possess a sense of female solidarity lacking in the *salonnières*, who remained isolated from one another by the primacy each held in her own salon. In an atmosphere of mutual support, the Bluestockings went beyond the salon experience. They traveled, studied, worked, wrote for publication, and by their activities challenged the stereotype of the passive woman. Although the *salonnières* were aware of sexual inequality, the narrow boundaries of their world kept their intellectual pursuits within conventional limits. Many *salonnières*, in fact, camouflaged their nontraditional activities behind the role of hostess and deferred to men in public.

Though the Bluestockings were trailblazers when compared with the *salonnières*, they were not feminists. They were too traditional, too hemmed in by their generation to demand social and political rights. Nonetheless, in their desire for education, their willingness to go beyond the confines of the salon in pursuing their interests, and their championing of unity among women, the Bluestockings began the process of questioning women's role in society.

17. Which of the following best states the central idea of the passage?

(A) The establishment of literary salons was a response to reformers' demands for social rights for women.

(B) Literary salons were originally intended to be a meeting ground for intellectuals of both sexes, but eventually became social gatherings with little educational value.

(C) In England, as in France, the general prejudice against higher education for women limited women's function in literary salons to a primarily social one.

(D) The literary salons provided a sounding board for French and English women who called for access to all the educational institutions in their societies on an equal basis with men.

(E) For women, who did not have access to higher education as men did, literary salons provided an alternate route to learning and a challenge to some of society's basic assumptions about women.

GO ON TO THE NEXT PAGE.

18. According to the passage, a significant distinction between the *salonnières* and Bluestockings was in the way each group regarded which of the following?

    (A) The value of acquiring knowledge
    (B) The role of pleasure in the activities of the literary salon
    (C) The desirability of a complete break with societal traditions
    (D) The inclusion of women of different backgrounds in the salons
    (E) The attainment of full social and political equality with men

19. The author refers to differences in social background between *salonnières* and Bluestockings in order to do which of the following?

    (A) Criticize the view that their choices of activities were significantly influenced by male salon members
    (B) Discuss the reasons why literary salons in France were established before those in England
    (C) Question the importance of the Bluestockings in shaping public attitudes toward educated women
    (D) Refute the argument that the French salons had little influence over the direction the English salons took
    (E) Explain the differences in atmosphere and style in their salons

20. Which of the following statements is most compatible with the principles of the *salonnières* as described in the passage?

    (A) Women should aspire to be not only educated but independent as well.
    (B) The duty of the educated woman is to provide an active political model for less educated women.
    (C) Devotion to pleasure and art is justified in itself.
    (D) Substance, rather than form, is the most important consideration in holding a literary salon.
    (E) Men should be excluded from groups of women's rights supporters.

21. The passage suggests that the Bluestockings might have had a more significant impact on society if it had not been for which of the following?

    (A) Competitiveness among their salons
    (B) Their emphasis on individualism
    (C) The limited scope of their activities
    (D) Their acceptance of the French salon as a model for their own salons
    (E) Their unwillingness to defy aggressively the conventions of their age

22. Which of the following could best be considered a twentieth-century counterpart of an eighteenth-century literary salon as it is described in the passage?

    (A) A social sorority
    (B) A community center
    (C) A lecture course on art
    (D) A humanities study group
    (E) An association of moral reformers

23. To an assertion that Bluestockings were feminists, the author would most probably respond with which of the following?

    (A) Admitted uncertainty
    (B) Qualified disagreement
    (C) Unquestioning approval
    (D) Complete indifference
    (E) Strong disparagement

24. Which of the following titles best describes the content of the passage?

    (A) Eighteenth-Century Egalitarianism
    (B) Feminists of the Eighteenth Century
    (C) Eighteenth-Century Precursors of Feminism
    (D) Intellectual Life in the Eighteenth Century
    (E) Female Education Reform in the Eighteenth Century

GO ON TO THE NEXT PAGE.

When the same parameters and quantitative theory are used to analyze both termite colonies and troops of rhesus macaques, we will have a unified science of sociobiology. Can this ever really happen? As my own studies have advanced, I have been increasingly impressed with the functional similarities between insect and vertebrate societies and less so with the structural differences that seem, at first glance, to constitute such an immense gulf between them. Consider for a moment termites and macaques. Both form cooperative groups that occupy territories. In both kinds of society there is a well-marked division of labor. Members of both groups communicate to each other hunger, alarm, hostility, caste status or rank, and reproductive status. From the specialist's point of view, this comparison may at first seem facile—or worse. But it is out of such deliberate oversimplification that the beginnings of a general theory are made.

25. Which of the following best summarizes the author's main point?

(A) Oversimplified comparisons of animal societies could diminish the likelihood of developing a unified science of socio-biology.

(B) Understanding the ways in which animals as different as termites and rhesus macaques resemble each other requires training in both biology and sociology.

(C) Most animals organize themselves into societies that exhibit patterns of group behavior similar to those of human societies.

(D) Animals as different as termites and rhesus macaques follow certain similar and predictable patterns of behavior.

(E) A study of the similarities between insect and vertebrate societies could provide the basis for a unified science of sociobiology.

26. The author's attitude toward the possibility of a unified theory in sociobiology is best described as which of the following?

(A) Guarded optimism
(B) Unqualified enthusiasm
(C) Objective indifference
(D) Resignation
(E) Dissatisfaction

27. In discussing insect and vertebrate societies, the author suggests which of the following?

(A) A distinguishing characteristic of most insect and vertebrate societies is a well-marked division of labor.

(B) The caste structure of insect societies is similar to that of vertebrate societies.

(C) Most insect and vertebrate societies form cooperative groups in order to occupy territory.

(D) The means of communication among members of insect societies is similar to that among members of vertebrate societies.

(E) There are significant structural differences between insect and vertebrate societies.

GO ON TO THE NEXT PAGE.

Directions: Each question below consists of a word printed in capital letters, followed by five lettered words or phrases. Choose the lettered word or phrase that is most nearly opposite in meaning to the word in capital letters.

Since some of the questions require you to distinguish fine shades of meaning, be sure to consider all the choices before deciding which one is best.

28. BEGIN: (A) participate (B) determine
    (C) persist (D) conclude (E) prevent

29. SHUN:
    (A) seek actively
    (B) perform occasionally
    (C) understand intuitively
    (D) answer correctly
    (E) influence easily

30. EQUITY: (A) uncleanness (B) unfairness
    (C) unskillfulness (D) unreadiness
    (E) unfaithfulness

31. PROPAGATION: (A) regulation
    (B) emulation (C) extirpation
    (D) infiltration (E) revelation

32. PRESUMPTUOUS: (A) delicate
    (B) humble (C) certain
    (D) constructive (E) contemptible

33. VACILLATION: (A) perpetual activity
    (B) rapid growth (C) motionless balance
    (D) accurate focus (E) minimal response

34. PENCHANT: (A) stigma (B) dishonesty
    (C) disbelief (D) grievance (E) dislike

35. SOMATIC: (A) unitary
    (B) disjointed (C) nonphysical
    (D) by hand (E) with effort

36. CONFOUND: (A) specify (B) signify
    (C) scrutinize (D) discriminate between
    (E) coincide with

37. CHARY: (A) brisk (B) bold
    (C) untidy (D) ungenerous (E) unfriendly

38. FLAG: (A) sustain (B) strive (C) favor
    (D) cut (E) wax

S T O P

IF YOU FINISH BEFORE TIME IS CALLED, YOU MAY CHECK YOUR WORK ON THIS SECTION ONLY.
DO NOT WORK ON ANY OTHER SECTION IN THE TEST.

SECTION 3
Time—30 minutes
30 Questions

Numbers: All numbers used are real numbers.

Figures: Position of points, angles, regions, etc. can be assumed to be in the order shown; and angle measures can be assumed to be positive.

Lines shown as straight can be assumed to be straight.

Figures can be assumed to lie in a plane unless otherwise indicated.

Figures that accompany questions are intended to provide information useful in answering the questions. However, unless a note states that a figure is drawn to scale, you should solve these problems NOT by estimating sizes by sight or by measurement, but by using your knowledge of mathematics (see Example 2 below).

Directions: Each of the Questions 1-15 consists of two quantities, one in Column A and one in Column B. You are to compare the two quantities and choose

A if the quantity in Column A is greater;
B if the quantity in Column B is greater;
C if the two quantities are equal;
D if the relationship cannot be determined from the information given.

Note: Since there are only four choices, NEVER MARK (E).

Common Information: In a question, information concerning one or both of the quantities to be compared is centered above the two columns. A symbol that appears in both columns represents the same thing in Column A as it does in Column B.

	Column A	Column B	Sample Answers
Example 1:	2×6	$2 + 6$	● Ⓑ Ⓒ Ⓓ Ⓔ

Examples 2-4 refer to $\triangle PQR$.

Example 2:	PN	NQ	Ⓐ Ⓑ Ⓒ ● Ⓔ

(since equal measures cannot be assumed, even though PN and NQ appear equal)

Example 3:	x	y	Ⓐ ● Ⓒ Ⓓ Ⓔ

(since N is between P and Q)

Example 4:	$w + z$	180	Ⓐ Ⓑ ● Ⓓ Ⓔ

(since PQ is a straight line)

GO ON TO THE NEXT PAGE.

A   if the quantity in Column A is greater;
B   if the quantity in Column B is greater;
C   if the two quantities are equal;
D   if the relationship cannot be determined from the information given.

	Column A	Column B
1.	1.76×100	0.176×10

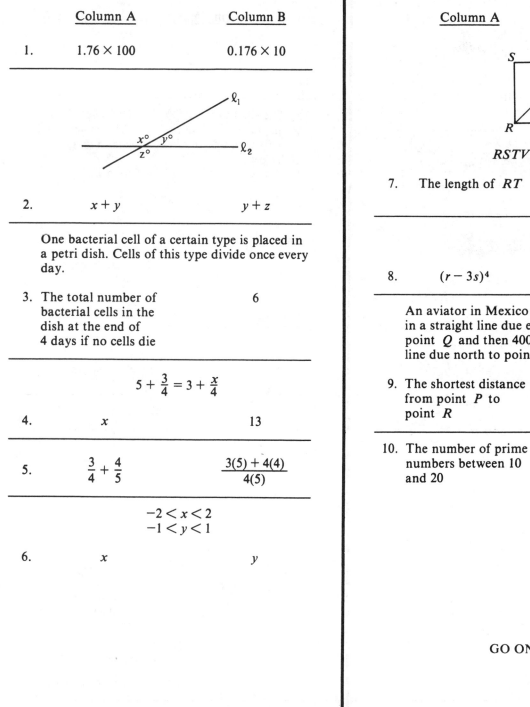

	Column A	Column B
2.	$x + y$	$y + z$

One bacterial cell of a certain type is placed in a petri dish. Cells of this type divide once every day.

3.	The total number of bacterial cells in the dish at the end of 4 days if no cells die	6

$$5 + \frac{3}{4} = 3 + \frac{x}{4}$$

4.	x	13

5.	$\frac{3}{4} + \frac{4}{5}$	$\frac{3(5) + 4(4)}{4(5)}$

$$-2 < x < 2$$
$$-1 < y < 1$$

6.	x	y

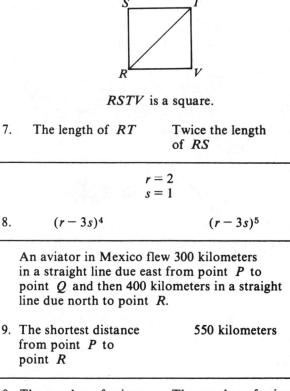

RSTV is a square.

	Column A	Column B
7.	The length of *RT*	Twice the length of *RS*

$$r = 2$$
$$s = 1$$

8.	$(r - 3s)^4$	$(r - 3s)^5$

An aviator in Mexico flew 300 kilometers in a straight line due east from point *P* to point *Q* and then 400 kilometers in a straight line due north to point *R*.

9.	The shortest distance from point *P* to point *R*	550 kilometers

10.	The number of prime numbers between 10 and 20	The number of prime numbers between 30 and 40

GO ON TO THE NEXT PAGE.

A   if the quantity in Column A is greater;
B   if the quantity in Column B is greater;
C   if the two quantities are equal;
D   if the relationship cannot be determined from the information given.

Column A	Column B

$$x > 0$$

11. The number of minutes in $x + 100$ hours   The number of seconds in $60(x + 100)$ minutes

---

12. $\sqrt{\dfrac{5}{2}}$ $\dfrac{1}{2}\sqrt{10}$

---

13. $(RS)^2 + (ST)^2$ $(RT)^2$

Column A	Column B

$$\sqrt{2x} = 4 \ \text{ and } \ y^2 = 64$$

14. x y

---

15. The length of the diagonal of a square with each side of length 2   The height of a triangle with each side of length 3

GO ON TO THE NEXT PAGE.

Directions: Each of the <u>Questions 16-30</u> has five answer choices. For each of these questions, select the best of the answer choices given.

---

16. $3 \times \frac{2}{2} =$

(A) $\frac{1}{3}$ (B) 1   (C) 3   (D) 6   (E) $6\frac{1}{2}$

17. If $k = 15$, then $\dfrac{(k-2)180}{k} =$

(A)   156
(B)   23
(C)   −23
(D) −204
(E) −360

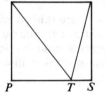

18. In the figure above, the area of square $PQRS$ is 64. What is the area of $\triangle QRT$?

(A) 48   (B) 32   (C) 24   (D) 16   (E) 8

19. If x equals 25 percent of a number, then 125 percent of the number is

(A) $\frac{x}{1.25}$ (B) $\frac{x}{4}$ (C) $1.25x$

(D) $4x$ (E) $5x$

20. If the cost of a long-distance phone call is c cents for the first minute and $\frac{2}{3}c$ cents for each additional minute, what is the cost, in cents, of a 10-minute call of this type?

(A) $\frac{5}{3}c$ (B) $6c$ (C) $\frac{20}{3}c$

(D) $7c$ (E) $\frac{23}{3}c$

GO ON TO THE NEXT PAGE.

Questions 21-25 refer to the following graphs.

PERCENT CONTRIBUTED TO PROFITS BY EACH OF THE
6 DIVISIONS, *P* THRU *U*, OF COMPANY Y FOR 1979 AND 1980

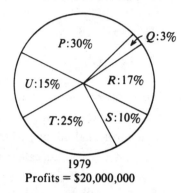

1979
Profits = $20,000,000

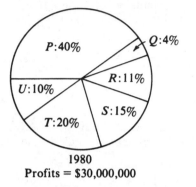

1980
Profits = $30,000,000

21. In 1980 what was the average of the amounts contributed to profits by Division *U* and Division *T*?

   (A) $1,000,000
   (B) $1,500,000
   (C) $3,000,000
   (D) $4,500,000
   (E) $6,500,000

22. Division *R* contributed how much less to the profits of Company *Y* in 1980 than in 1979 ?

   (A) $600,000
   (B) $300,000
   (C) $180,000
   (D) $120,000
   (E) $100,000

23. In 1979 the greatest contribution to profits by one of the six divisions was what percent of the least contribution?

   (A) 10%   (B) 90%   (C) 100%

   (D) 900%   (E) 1,000%

24. If the six divisions are ranked each year according to their dollar contributions to profits, from greatest contribution to lowest, how many divisions ranked lower in 1980 than in 1979 ?

   (A) None
   (B) One
   (C) Two
   (D) Three
   (E) Four

25. How many of the divisions contributed more dollars to profits in 1980 than in 1979 ?

   (A) One
   (B) Two
   (C) Three
   (D) Four
   (E) Five

GO ON TO THE NEXT PAGE.

26. In a certain apartment building exactly $\frac{1}{3}$ of the apartments have two bedrooms and exactly $\frac{1}{7}$ of the two-bedroom apartments are front apartments. Which of the following could be the total number of apartments in the building?

(A) 42
(B) 50
(C) 51
(D) 56
(E) 57

27. Which of the following could be the area of an isosceles triangle with perimeter 18 and one side of length 8 ?

(A) 6
(B) 12
(C) 14
(D) 16
(E) 18

28. When a certain number is divided by 7, the remainder is 0. If the remainder is <u>not</u> 0 when the number is divided by 14, then the remainder must be

(A) 1   (B) 2   (C) 4   (D) 6   (E) 7

29. If $x > 0$ and $2x - 1 = \frac{1}{2x + 1}$, then $x =$

(A) $\frac{1}{2}$

(B) $\frac{\sqrt{2}}{2}$

(C) 1

(D) $\sqrt{2}$

(E) $\sqrt{2} + 1$

30. If the radius of a circle is decreased by 30 percent, by what percent will the area of the circular region be decreased?

(A) 15%
(B) 49%
(C) 51%
(D) 60%
(E) 90%

S T O P

IF YOU FINISH BEFORE TIME IS CALLED, YOU MAY CHECK YOUR WORK ON THIS SECTION ONLY.
DO NOT WORK ON ANY OTHER SECTION IN THE TEST.

SECTION 4
Time—30 minutes
30 Questions

Numbers: All numbers used are real numbers.

Figures: Position of points, angles, regions, etc. can be assumed to be in the order shown; and angle measures can be assumed to be positive.

Lines shown as straight can be assumed to be straight.

Figures can be assumed to lie in a plane unless otherwise indicated.

Figures that accompany questions are intended to provide information useful in answering the questions. However, unless a note states that a figure is drawn to scale, you should solve these problems NOT by estimating sizes by sight or by measurement, but by using your knowledge of mathematics (see Example 2 below).

Directions: Each of the Questions 1-15 consists of two quantities, one in Column A and one in Column B. You are to compare the two quantities and choose

A if the quantity in Column A is greater;
B if the quantity in Column B is greater;
C if the two quantities are equal;
D if the relationship cannot be determined from the information given.

Note: Since there are only four choices, NEVER MARK (E).

Common Information: In a question, information concerning one or both of the quantities to be compared is centered above the two columns. A symbol that appears in both columns represents the same thing in Column A as it does in Column B.

	Column A	Column B	Sample Answers
Example 1:	2×6	$2 + 6$	● Ⓑ Ⓒ Ⓓ Ⓔ

Examples 2-4 refer to $\triangle PQR$.

Example 2:	PN	NQ	Ⓐ Ⓑ Ⓒ ● Ⓔ

(since equal measures cannot be assumed, even though PN and NQ appear equal)

Example 3:	x	y	Ⓐ ● Ⓒ Ⓓ Ⓔ

(since N is between P and Q)

Example 4:	$w + z$	180	Ⓐ Ⓑ ● Ⓓ Ⓔ

(since PQ is a straight line)

GO ON TO THE NEXT PAGE.

A if the quantity in Column A is greater;
B if the quantity in Column B is greater;
C if the two quantities are equal;
D if the relationship cannot be determined from the information given.

	Column A	Column B
1.	$2(10^3) + 5(10^2) + 7$	257

$$7n + x = 23$$
$$n = 3$$

	Column A	Column B
2.	x	n

3.	$\frac{1}{4}$ of 5	$\frac{1}{5}$ of 4

$$0 < x < y$$

4.	$x - y$	$y - x$

5.	The number of bonds that were purchased for $2,500	The number of bonds that were purchased for $3,500

6.	The volume of a sphere that has radius 4	The volume of a sphere that has diameter 8

a, b, and c are consecutive odd integers, not necessarily in that order.

7.	$a - b$	$b - c$

Column A   Column B

The length of PR is 12.

8.	The length of QS	8

$$x = -|x|$$
$$x \neq 0$$

9.	x	0

The altitude of a certain triangular sail is 2 meters greater in length than its base. The area of the face of the sail is 24 square meters.

10.	The length of the base of the sail	4 meters

GO ON TO THE NEXT PAGE.

137

A if the quantity in Column A is greater;
B if the quantity in Column B is greater;
C if the two quantities are equal;
D if the relationship cannot be determined from the information given.

Column A	Column B
11. $(-1)^{77} (-2)^3$	8

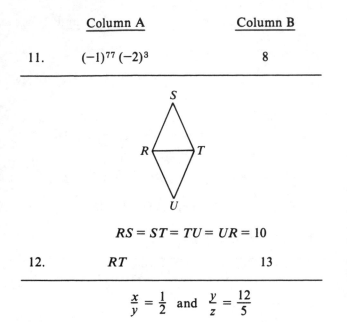

$$RS = ST = TU = UR = 10$$

	Column A	Column B
12.	RT	13

$$\frac{x}{y} = \frac{1}{2} \quad \text{and} \quad \frac{y}{z} = \frac{12}{5}$$

x, y, and z are positive numbers.

	Column A	Column B
13.	x	z

	Column A	Column B
14.	The area of a circular region with diameter x	The area of a square region with diagonal of length x

On July 1 the ratio of men to women in Club X was 9 to 20. During the month, 2 additional men and 2 additional women joined the club, and no members dropped out.

	Column A	Column B
15.	The ratio of men to women in Club X at the end of July	$\frac{1}{2}$

GO ON TO THE NEXT PAGE.

Directions: Each of the Questions 16-30 has five answer choices. For each of these questions, select the best of the answer choices given.

16. If $x = 3$ is one solution to the equation $x^2 + rx - 20 = 4$, then $r =$

   (A) -8
   (B) -5
   (C) -3
   (D) 5
   (E) 8

17. If the value of a certain fraction is equal to 0.4 and the denominator of the fraction is 15, then the numerator of the fraction is

   (A) 6
   (B) 8
   (C) 9
   (D) 12
   (E) 37.5

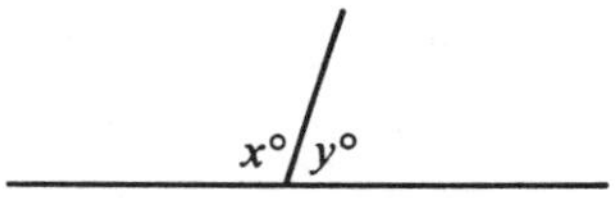

18. In the figure above, the ratio of x to y is 3 to 2. What is the value of y ?

   (A) 108   (B) 72   (C) 36   (D) 3   (E) 2

19. What was the original price of an item if a discount of 20 percent reduced the price to $100 ?

   (A) $80
   (B) $120
   (C) $125
   (D) $150
   (E) $250

20. The number of connections C that can be made through a switchboard to which T telephones are connected is given by the formula $C = \dfrac{T(T-1)}{2}$. How many more connections are possible with 30 telephones than with 20 telephones?

   (A) 435   (B) 245   (C) 190
   (D) 45   (E) 10

GO ON TO THE NEXT PAGE.

Questions 21-25 refer to the following graph.

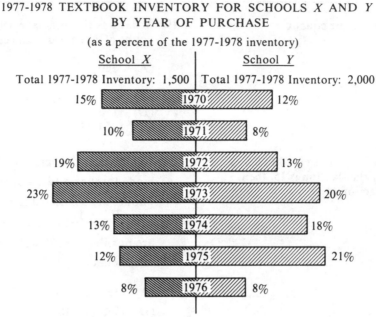

1977-1978 TEXTBOOK INVENTORY FOR SCHOOLS *X* AND *Y*
BY YEAR OF PURCHASE
(as a percent of the 1977-1978 inventory)

School *X*   School *Y*

Total 1977-1978 Inventory: 1,500 | Total 1977-1978 Inventory: 2,000

15%	1970	12%
10%	1971	8%
19%	1972	13%
23%	1973	20%
13%	1974	18%
12%	1975	21%
8%	1976	8%

Note: All books were purchased new on July 1 of each year.

21. What percent of School *Y*'s 1977-1978 textbook inventory was bought in 1975 ?

   (A)   9%
   (B)   12%
   (C)   21%
   (D)   33%
   (E)   It cannot be determined from the information given.

22. In School *X* how many of the inventoried textbooks were purchased prior to 1976 ?

   (A) 100   (B) 120   (C) 140
   (D) 1,340   (E) 1,380

23. How many of the inventoried textbooks were purchased by the two schools combined during the years 1974, 1975, and 1976 ?

   (A)   495
   (B)   940
   (C) 1,020
   (D) 1,435
   (E) 2,800

24. If School *X* purchased 300 textbooks in 1971 and all of these textbooks either were counted in the inventory or had been discarded before the inventory, what percent of these textbooks had been discarded?

   (A)   10%
   (B)   20%
   (C)   50%
   (D)   80%
   (E) 100%

25. Which of the following statements can be inferred from the graph?

   I.   School *X* has a smaller enrollment than School *Y*.
   II. If the age of a book is the number of years since purchase, then the average (arithmetic mean) age of a book in the School *Y* inventory is less than that of a book in the School *X* inventory.
   III. According to the inventory, School *X* and School *Y* purchased the same number of textbooks in 1976.

   (A) None   (B) I only   (C) II only
   (D) I and II   (E) II and III

GO ON TO THE NEXT PAGE.

26. If $\frac{2}{3}$ of the number of women attending a certain dance is equal to $\frac{1}{2}$ the number of men attending, what fraction of those attending are women?

(A) $\frac{2}{5}$

(B) $\frac{3}{7}$

(C) $\frac{5}{7}$

(D) $\frac{3}{4}$

(E) $\frac{5}{6}$

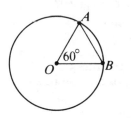

27. In the figure above, O is the center of the circle. If $AB = 10$, what is the area of the circle?

(A) 10π (B) 20π (C) 25π

(D) 50π (E) 100π

28. How many of the positive integers less than 25 are 2 less than an integer multiple of 4 ?

(A) Two
(B) Three
(C) Four
(D) Five
(E) Six

29. If $7x - 4y = -1$ and $5x + 3y = 52$, then $x - y =$

(A) -4
(B) -3
(C) 3
(D) 4
(E) 5

30. The floor of a company's storage room has an area of 20,000 square feet. If the floor is in the shape of a square, approximately how many feet long is each side?

(A) 140   (B) 450   (C) 500
(D) 1,000   (E) 5,000

S T O P

IF YOU FINISH BEFORE TIME IS CALLED, YOU MAY CHECK YOUR WORK ON THIS SECTION ONLY.
DO NOT WORK ON ANY OTHER SECTION IN THE TEST.

SECTION 5

Time—30 minutes

25 Questions

Directions: Each question or group of questions is based on a passage or set of conditions. In answering some of the questions, it may be useful to draw a rough diagram. For each question, select the best answer choice given.

Questions 1-4

All padlocks manufactured by the Guaranteed Combination Lock Company have a combination that consists of four elements—a one-digit number, a two-digit number, and two letters of the alphabet. Each combination conforms to the following rules:

(1)   The one-digit number is the first element in the combination.

(2)   The two letters of the alphabet are not adjacent elements in the combination.

(3)   The two-digit number consists of two different numerals.

(4)   The two-digit number has no numerals in common with the one-digit number.

1. Which of the following is a sequence of elements that conforms to the rules?

   (A)   6-73-D-M
   (B)   2-X-37-G
   (C)   39-H-Y-6
   (D)   H-24-K-4
   (E)   9-B-89-B

2. Which of the following must always be true of a combination?

   (A)   The second element is a two-digit number.
   (B)   The third element is a letter of the alphabet.
   (C)   The third element is a one-digit number.
   (D)   The fourth element is a two-digit number.
   (E)   The fourth element is a letter of the alphabet.

3. Which of the following CANNOT be the first element of a combination that has K-53-J as its second, third, and fourth elements?

   (A)   5
   (B)   6
   (C)   7
   (D)   8
   (E)   9

4. The sequence of elements 9-K-M-29 violates which of the rules given?

   (A)   Rule 2 only
   (B)   Rule 3 only
   (C)   Rule 2 and rule 4 only
   (D)   Rule 3 and rule 4 only
   (E)   Rule 2, rule 3, and rule 4

GO ON TO THE NEXT PAGE.

5. If your radio was made after 1972, it has a stereo feature.

The statement above can be deduced logically from which of the following statements?

(A) Only if a radio was made after 1972 could it have a stereo feature.

(B) All radios made after 1972 have a stereo feature.

(C) Some radios made before 1972 had a stereo feature.

(D) Some stereo features are found in radios made after 1972.

(E) Stereo features for radios were fully developed only after 1972.

6. Rule 1 of Game X provides that anyone who refuses to become a player in Game X shall at the moment of refusal be assessed a ten-point penalty in the game.

Which of the following claims is implicit in Rule 1?

(A) All those who agree to play Game X will achieve scores higher than the scores of those who were assessed a penalty under Rule 1.

(B) A person can avoid a ten-point penalty by initially agreeing to become a player and then withdrawing after the game is under way.

(C) The rules of Game X supply a procedure for determining when the game is over.

(D) A person who refuses to play Game X cannot be declared a loser in the game.

(E) A person can at the same time decline to play Game X and yet be a part of the game.

7. A common misconception is that university hospitals are better than community or private hospitals. In fact, university hospitals have a lower survival rate for patients than do other hospitals. From this it seems clear that the quality of care at university hospitals is lower than that at other hospitals.

Which of the following, if true, most forcefully undermines the argument of the passage above?

(A) Many doctors divide their working hours between a university and a community or private hospital.

(B) Doctors at university hospitals often earn less than doctors at private hospitals.

(C) University and community hospitals often cannot afford the elaborate facilities of private hospitals.

(D) The emphasis at many university hospitals is on pure research rather than on the treatment and care of patients.

(E) The patients who seek help at university hospitals are usually more seriously ill than those at private or community hospitals.

GO ON TO THE NEXT PAGE.

Questions 8-11

A pet store owner is setting up several fish tanks, each to contain exactly six fish so chosen from species F, G, H, I, J, K, and L that none of the fish in any given tank will fight. Fish of any of the species above can be placed in a tank together except for the following restrictions:

    Fish of species F will fight with fish of species H, J, and K.

    Fish of species I will fight with fish of species G and K.

    If three or more fish of species I are in one tank, they will fight with each other.

    Fish of species J will fight with fish of species L.

    If a fish of species G is to be in a tank, at least one fish of species K must also be in the tank.

8. If a tank is to contain fish of exactly three different species, these species could be

    (A) F, G, and I   (B) F, I, and K
    (C) G, H, and I   (D) H, I, and J
    (E) I, J, and L

9. If there are to be exactly two species represented in a tank, and three fish of species J are to be in the tank, the other three fish in that tank could be from which of the following species?

    (A) F   (B) G   (C) H   (D) I   (E) L

10. If a tank is to contain fish of exactly four different species, it CANNOT contain fish of species

    (A) F   (B) G   (C) H   (D) J   (E) L

11. Fish of which of the following species could be put into a tank with fish of species G ?

    (A) F and I   (B) F and J   (C) H and I
    (D) H and K   (E) I and K

GO ON TO THE NEXT PAGE.

Questions 12-17

Two circular dials of exactly the same size are mounted on a wall side by side in such a way that their perimeters touch at one point.

Dial 1, which is on the left, spins clockwise around its center, and dial 2, which is on the right, spins counterclockwise around its center. (Assume that there is no friction at the point of contact between the dials.)

Each dial has marked on its perimeter three points that are at equal distances around the perimeter from each other.

Going clockwise on each dial the points marked on dial 1 are N, O, and P, and the points marked on dial 2 are X, Y, and Z.

12. Which of the following lists the points on a dial in an order in which they could pass consecutively through the point of contact between the dials?

   (A) O, N, P   (B) O, P, O   (C) X, Z, Y
   (D) Y, X, Z   (E) Z, X, Z

13. If points O and Z are just meeting at the point of contact between the dials, and if dial 1 spins at the same speed as dial 2, what is the smallest number of revolutions of each dial that will bring O and Z together again?

   (A) 1   (B) 2   (C) 3   (D) 4   (E) 5

14. If points N and Y are just meeting at the point of contact between the dials, and if dial 1 spins at the same speed as dial 2, which of the following pairs of points will also meet in the course of the next full revolution of the dials?

   (A) N and Z   (B) O and X   (C) O and Z
   (D) P and X   (E) P and Y

15. Which of the following is a possible sequence of pairs of points meeting consecutively at the point of contact between the dials if dial 1 spins at the same speed as dial 2 ?

   (A) N and O followed by X and Z
   (B) N and X followed by O and Z
   (C) O and X followed by N and X
   (D) O and Y followed by N and Z
   (E) P and Z followed by P and X

16. If points P and X are just meeting at the point of contact between the dials, and if dial 2 spins at exactly double the speed of dial 1, which of the following pairs of points will be the next pair to meet at the point of contact?

   (A) N and Y   (B) N and Z   (C) O and X
   (D) O and Z   (E) P and Y

17. If points P and Y are just meeting at the point of contact between the dials, and if dial 1 spins at exactly three times the speed of dial 2, which of the following pairs of points will be the next pair to meet at the point of contact?

   (A) N and X   (B) N and Z   (C) O and Y
   (D) P and X   (E) P and Z

GO ON TO THE NEXT PAGE.

145

Questions 18-22

Ten different fabrics are being displayed on racks along one wall of a store. The racks are next to each other in a straight line and are numbered consecutively from one to ten. On each rack is a single bolt of a different fabric. One fabric is green, two fabrics are different shades of brown, three fabrics are different shades of purple, and the remaining four fabrics are different shades of red.

> Purple fabrics are on racks one and ten.
> The two brown fabrics are on racks next to each other.
> No red fabric is on a rack next to a brown fabric.
> No purple fabric is on a rack next to the green fabric.

18. If a purple fabric is on rack two and red fabrics are on racks three and four, the green fabric must be on which of the following racks?

    (A) Five   (B) Six   (C) Seven
    (D) Eight   (E) Nine

19. If the four red fabrics are on four consecutive racks, the green fabric and one of the brown fabrics could be on which of the following racks, respectively?

    (A) Two and three   (B) Three and four
    (C) Four and five   (D) Five and six
    (E) Six and seven

20. Which of the following are colors of fabrics that CANNOT be on racks two, three, and four, respectively?

    (A) Purple, red, green
    (B) Purple, brown, brown
    (C) Brown, brown, purple
    (D) Red, red, green
    (E) Red, red, red

21. If a purple fabric is on rack three and a brown fabric is on rack four, the green fabric must be on which of the following racks?

    (A) Two   (B) Five   (C) Six
    (D) Seven   (E) Nine

22. If the green fabric is on rack five and a brown fabric is on rack four, which of the following must be true?

    (A) A red fabric is on rack two.
    (B) A red fabric is on rack nine.
    (C) A purple fabric is on rack six.
    (D) A purple fabric is on rack seven.
    (E) A purple fabric is on rack eight.

---

23. Literary historians today have rejected conventional analyses of the development of English Renaissance drama. They no longer accept the idea that the sudden achievement of Elizabethan playwrights was a historical anomaly, a sort of magical rediscovery of ancient Greek dramatic form applied to contemporary English subject matter. Instead, most students of the theater now view Elizabethan drama as being organically related to traditional local drama, particularly medieval morality plays.

    Which of the following is NOT consistent with the passage above?

    (A) England had a dramatic tradition before the Renaissance period.
    (B) Elizabethan drama, once thought to be a sudden blossoming forth of creativity, is now seen as part of a historical continuum.
    (C) Historians' views of the antecedents of English Renaissance drama have changed considerably.
    (D) Current scholarship applies an evolutionary model to English Renaissance drama.
    (E) Although English Renaissance drama treats English subject matter, its source of form and method is classical Greek drama.

GO ON TO THE NEXT PAGE.

24. In 1975, 35 percent of state W's work force was employed in manufacturing jobs. That percentage dropped in each following year until in 1982 it reached 25 percent.

    If the statements above are true, all of the following statements about changes in W's work force between 1975 and 1982 could also be true EXCEPT:

    (A) The number of people in the work force increased, while the number of people employed in manufacturing jobs decreased.
    (B) The number of people in the work force decreased, while the number of people employed in manufacturing jobs increased.
    (C) Both the number of people in the work force and the number of people employed in manufacturing jobs increased.
    (D) Both the number of people in the work force and the number of people employed in manufacturing jobs decreased.
    (E) The number of people in the work force remained constant, while the number of people employed in manufacturing jobs decreased.

25. The excessive number of safety regulations that the federal government has placed on industry poses more serious hardships for big businesses than for small ones. Since large companies do everything on a more massive scale, they must alter more complex operations and spend much more money to meet governmental requirements.

    Which of the following, if true, would most weaken the argument above?

    (A) Small companies are less likely than large companies to have the capital reserves for improvements.
    (B) The operations of small companies frequently rely on the same technologies as the operations of large companies.
    (C) Safety regulation codes are uniform, established without reference to size of company.
    (D) Large companies typically have more of their profits invested in other businesses than do small companies.
    (E) Large companies are in general more likely than small companies to diversify their markets and products.

S T O P

IF YOU FINISH BEFORE TIME IS CALLED, YOU MAY CHECK YOUR WORK ON THIS SECTION ONLY.
DO NOT WORK ON ANY OTHER SECTION IN THE TEST.

SECTION 6

Time—30 minutes

25 Questions

Directions: Each question or group of questions is based on a passage or set of conditions. In answering some of the questions, it may be useful to draw a rough diagram. For each question, select the best answer choice given.

Questions 1-4

Seats on a small plane are being assigned to six passengers—N, P, Q, R, S, and T. The eight seats on the plane are in four rows, numbered 1 through 4, and each row has two seats. Seat assignments are made according to the following conditions:

N must sit alone in a row.
P must sit in the same row as R.
Q cannot sit in the same row as S.
The rows with only one passenger must be row 1 and row 3.

1. Which of the following passengers could be assigned to sit in the same row as Q ?

(A) N
(B) P
(C) R
(D) S
(E) T

2. If P and R are in row 2, which of the following must be true?

(A) N is in row 1.
(B) Q is in row 1.
(C) Q is in row 4.
(D) S is in row 3.
(E) T is in row 4.

3. Which of the following is the total number of passengers eligible to be the passenger assigned to sit in the same row as T ?

(A) 1
(B) 2
(C) 3
(D) 4
(E) 5

4. If Q and T are assigned to sit together in a row, which of the following passengers could be assigned to sit in row 3 ?

(A) P
(B) Q
(C) R
(D) S
(E) T

GO ON TO THE NEXT PAGE.

5. Public education suffers from what can be diagnosed as the sickness of an overgoverned society. This sickness denies many parents control over the kind of education their children receive. The power once held by parents has gravitated to professional educators. The sickness has been aggravated by increasing centralization and bureaucratization of schools.

Which of the following, if true, would weaken the claim that there is continuing erosion of parents' control over their children's education?

(A) As a result of community pressure, growing numbers of school administrators follow recommendations made by parents.
(B) The number of professional educators has risen sharply over the last decade even though the number of students has declined.
(C) Parents' organizations that lobby for changes in school curriculums are generally ineffectual.
(D) More members of school boards are appointed by school administrators than are elected by the public.
(E) The use of state-wide curriculum programs increased in the United States during the past two decades.

6. From a certain farming region, trucks can carry vegetables to market in New Mexico in two days for a total cost of $300. A train will carry the vegetables there in four days for $200. If reducing time in transit is more important to the owner of the vegetables than is reducing the shipping bill, he or she will send the vegetables by truck.

Which of the following is an assumption made in the passage above?

(A) Vegetables can be sold more profitably when shipped by train than by truck.
(B) Other than speed and cost, there are no significant differences between truck and train transportation from the farming region to New Mexico.
(C) The time required to ship vegetables by train from the farming region to New Mexico could be reduced to two days if the price for this service were raised.
(D) Most owners of vegetables in the region are more concerned with shipping costs than with the time involved in shipping vegetables to market.
(E) Transportation of vegetables by truck is worth at least $200 per day to owners of the vegetables in the farming region.

7. The expression "the doctrine of unshakable foundations" was once used by a critic in an effort to illuminate the dogmatic nature of certain economic and political philosophies whose adherents, when confronted with the failure of a policy designed to put their philosophy into practice, can conceive of only one reaction: to design another, different policy for putting it into practice.

It can be inferred from the passage above that the critic would approve if the adherents

(A) had the courage to try a failed policy again without any changes
(B) had refrained from trying to put any of their philosophies into practice
(C) allowed failure of a policy to lead them to question the underpinnings of their philosophies
(D) concluded from the failure of a policy of theirs that the policy must not have reflected their philosophy adequately
(E) carefully analyzed those traits of a failed policy that appear promising despite the overall failure

GO ON TO THE NEXT PAGE.

Questions 8-13

The members of the Public Service Commission and the members of the Rent Control Commission are to be selected from exactly six qualified candidates. The six candidates are U, V, W, X, Y, and Z. The following rules apply:

Each commission must have exactly three members.
The two commissions must have at least one member in common.
U cannot be on a commission with X.
If X is selected for a commission, Y must also be selected for that commission.

8. If the members of the Public Service Commission are selected first, which of the following could be those selected?

   (A) U, V, and X
   (B) U, X, and Z
   (C) V, W, and X
   (D) V, X, and Y
   (E) W, X, and Z

9. If the two commissions have parallel terms of office, which of the following could be selected as the members of the Public Service Commission and as the members of the Rent Control Commission, respectively, for one such term of office?

   (A) U, V, and W; X, Y, and Z
   (B) U, W, and Y; V, X, and Z
   (C) U, X, and Y; U, X, and Z
   (D) V, W, and Y; V, W, and X
   (E) W, X, and Y; X, Y, and Z

10. If the members of the Public Service Commission are V, W, and Z, and if the Rent Control Commission is to have as many members in common with the Public Service Commission as the rules allow, the Rent Control Commission must consist of

   (A) U, V, and W
   (B) V, W, and Z
   (C) V, X, and Z
   (D) W, Y, and Z
   (E) X, Y, and Z

11. If U, V, and W make up the Public Service Commission, and W, Y, and Z make up the Rent Control Commission, which of these commission members could yield his or her place on a commission to X without necessitating any other membership changes?

   (A) U
   (B) V
   (C) W
   (D) Y
   (E) Z

12. If U and X are each selected for a commission, and only Z is selected for both commissions, which of the following must be true?

   (A) V is selected for the same commission as W.
   (B) W is selected for the same commission as Y.
   (C) W is selected for the same commission as X.
   (D) U is selected for a different commission than Y.
   (E) X is selected for a different commission than Y.

13. If X and Z are both selected for the Public Service Commission, and if U is selected for the Rent Control Commission, each of the following pairs of people could be the other two members of the Rent Control Commission EXCEPT

   (A) V and W
   (B) V and Z
   (C) W and Y
   (D) W and Z
   (E) Y and Z

GO ON TO THE NEXT PAGE.

Questions 14-17

A variety show producer is auditioning five performers in five consecutive auditions. Each performer auditions alone, and only once. The five performers are: two singers (a tenor and a soprano), a dancer, a magician, and a comedian. The auditions must be scheduled according to the following conditions:

The two singers cannot audition one after the other.

The magician must audition immediately before a singer.

The comedian must audition immediately before or immediately after the dancer.

14. If the comedian auditions first, which of the following must be true?

   (A) The soprano auditions third.
   (B) The magician auditions fourth.
   (C) The tenor auditions fifth.
   (D) The soprano auditions sometime earlier than the dancer.
   (E) The dancer auditions immediately before the tenor.

15. If the tenor auditions first, and the soprano auditions fifth, which of the following must be true?

   (A) The comedian auditions sometime after the magician.
   (B) The comedian auditions immediately after the dancer.
   (C) The magician auditions sometime after the dancer.
   (D) The magician auditions sometime before the comedian.
   (E) The dancer auditions immediately before the magician.

16. If the comedian, the soprano, and the magician audition one after the other, in that order, which of the following must be true?

   (A) The comedian is the first of the five to audition.
   (B) The soprano is the second of the five to audition.
   (C) The magician is the third of the five to audition.
   (D) The dancer is the fourth of the five to audition.
   (E) The tenor is the fifth of the five to audition.

17. If the magician auditions sometime earlier than the dancer, a singer CANNOT audition in which of the following positions?

   (A) First
   (B) Second
   (C) Third
   (D) Fourth
   (E) Fifth

GO ON TO THE NEXT PAGE.

Questions 18-22

On an island there are exactly seven towns: T, U, V, W, X, Y, and Z. All existing and projected roads on the island are two-way and run perfectly straight between one town and the next. All distances by road are distances from the main square of one town to the main square of another town. U is the same distance by road from T, V, and W as Y is from X and Z. The following are all of the currently existing roads and connections by road on the island:

Road 1 goes from T to V via U.
Road 2 goes from U directly to W.
The Triangle Road goes from X to Y, from Y on to Z, and from Z back to X.
Any main square reached by two roads is an interchange between them, and there are no other interchanges between roads.

18. Which of the following is a town from which exactly two other towns can be reached by road?

    (A) T   (B) U   (C) V   (D) W   (E) X

19. It is possible that the distance by road from X to Y is <u>unequal</u> to the distance by road from

    (A) T to U   (B) U to V   (C) U to W
    (D) X to Z   (E) Y to Z

20. Which of the following is a pair of towns connected by two routes by road that have no stretch of road in common?

    (A) T and U   (B) U and V   (C) V and W
    (D) W and X   (E) X and Y

21. If a projected road from T to Y were built, then the shortest distance by road from W to X would be the same as the shortest distance by road from Z to

    (A) T   (B) U   (C) V   (D) X   (E) Y

22. If two projected roads were built, one from T directly to Y and one from V directly to Z, then each of the following would be a complete list of the towns lying along one of the routes that a traveler going by road from U to X could select EXCEPT

    (A) T, Y   (B) T, Z   (C) V, Z
    (D) T, Y, Z   (E) V, Z, Y

---

23. If an investment has produced no profit, tax relief predicated on having made the investment is no help; any corporate manager who fears that a new asset will not make money is scarcely comforted by promises of reductions in taxes the corporation will not owe.

Which of the following is the most reliable inference to draw from the passage above?

(A) An effective way to discourage unprofitable corporate investment is to predicate tax relief on the making of profitable investments.

(B) Corporate managers are likely to ignore tax considerations in deciding to invest in assets they believe will be profitable.

(C) The promise of tax benefits for making new investments will not in and of itself stimulate new investment.

(D) The less importance a corporate manager attaches to tax considerations, the more likely it is that the manager will accurately predict the profitability of an investment.

(E) The critical factor in a corporate investment decision is likely to be a corporate manager's emotional response to perceived business conditions.

GO ON TO THE NEXT PAGE.

24. The results of a recent poll in the United States indicate that the public, by 80 percent to 17 percent, opposes relaxation of existing regulation of air pollution. Furthermore, not a single major segment of the public wants environmental laws made less strict. The results of this poll reveal that legislators, by voting for renewal of the Clean Air Act, will be responsive to the will of the public without alienating any significant special-interest groups.

Which of the following pieces of information would be most useful in evaluating the logic of the argument presented above?

(A) The groups in the population that were defined as major segments of the public and the groups defined as special-interest groups
(B) The length of time that current federal environmental laws have been in effect and the length of time that states have regulated air pollution
(C) The probable economic effect of renewal of the Clean Air Act on those opposed to and those in favor of relaxing environmental laws
(D) The people whom the author hopes to influence by citing the results of the poll
(E) The percentage of those surveyed who chose not to respond to the questions asked of them

25. After a rebellion in a certain country was put down, the country's parliament debated how to deal with the defeated rebels. One side proposed that all the rebels be imprisoned in order to deter those who might be strongly tempted to rebel in the future. The other side argued against imprisonment because it would only discourage future insurrectionists from surrendering.

Both positions logically depend on the assumption that

(A) imprisonment is a harsh penalty
(B) a rebel will prefer a sentence of imprisonment to death
(C) there will be no future rebellion in the country
(D) it is unlikely that future rebels will surrender
(E) resistance to authority is weakened by harsh threats

S T O P

IF YOU FINISH BEFORE TIME IS CALLED, YOU MAY CHECK YOUR WORK ON THIS SECTION ONLY.
DO NOT WORK ON ANY OTHER SECTION IN THE TEST.

THE GRADUATE RECORD EXAMINATIONS
GENERAL TEST

You will have 3 hours and 30 minutes in which to work on this test, which consists of seven sections. During the time allowed for one section, you may work only on that section. The time allowed for each section is 30 minutes.

Your score will be based on the number of questions for which you select the best answer choice given. No deduction will be made for a question for which you do not select the best answer choice given. Therefore, you are advised to answer all questions.

You are advised to work as rapidly as you can without losing accuracy. Do not spend too much time on questions that are too difficult for you. Go on to the other questions and come back to the difficult ones later.

There are several different types of questions; you will find special directions for each type in the test itself. Be sure you understand the directions before attempting to answer any questions.

For each question several answer choices (lettered A-E or A-D) are given from which you are to select the ONE best answer. YOU MUST INDICATE ALL OF YOUR ANSWERS ON THE SEPARATE ANSWER SHEET. No credit will be given for anything written in this examination book, but to work out your answers you may write in the book as much as you wish. After you have decided which of the suggested answers is best, blacken the corresponding space on the answer sheet. Be sure to:

- Use a soft black lead pencil (No. 2 or HB).

- Mark only one answer to each question. No credit will be given for multiple answers.

- Mark your answer in the row with the same number as the number of the question you are answering.

- Carefully and completely blacken the space corresponding to the answer you select for each question. Fill the space with a dark mark so that you cannot see the letter inside the space. Light or partial marks may not be read by the scoring machine. See the example of proper and improper answer marks below.

- Erase all stray marks. If you change an answer, be sure that you completely erase the old answer before marking your new answer. Incomplete erasures may be read as intended answers.

Example:

What city is the capital of France?

(A) Rome
(B) Paris
(C) London
(D) Cairo
(E) Oslo

Sample Answer

Ⓐ ● Ⓒ Ⓓ Ⓔ   BEST ANSWER
                PROPERLY MARKED

Ⓐ ⊗ Ⓒ Ⓓ Ⓔ
Ⓐ ⊘ Ⓒ Ⓓ Ⓔ   IMPROPER MARKS
Ⓐ ⊕ Ⓒ Ⓓ Ⓔ
Ⓐ ◑ Ⓒ Ⓓ Ⓔ

Do not be concerned that the answer sheet provides spaces for more answers than there are questions in the test. Some or all of the passages for this test have been adapted from published material to provide the examinee with significant problems for analysis and evaluation. To make the passages suitable for testing purposes, the style, content, or point of view of the original may have been altered in some cases. The ideas contained in the passages do not necessarily represent the opinions of the Graduate Record Examinations Board or Educational Testing Service.

CLOSE YOUR TEST BOOK AND WAIT FOR FURTHER INSTRUCTIONS FROM THE SUPERVISOR.

I

NOTE: To ensure the prompt and accurate processing of test results, your cooperation in following these directions is needed. The procedures that follow have been kept to the minimum necessary. They will take a few minutes to complete, but it is essential that you fill in all blanks <u>exactly</u> as directed.

GENERAL TEST

A. Print and sign your full name in this box:

PRINT: _____
(LAST)   (FIRST)   (MIDDLE)

SIGN: _____

B. Your answer sheet contains areas which will be used to ensure accurate reporting of your test results. It is essential that you fill in these areas <u>exactly</u> as explained below.

[1] YOUR NAME, MAILING ADDRESS, AND TEST CENTER: Place your answer sheet so that the heading "Graduate Record Examinations—General Test" is at the top. In box 1 below that heading <u>print</u> your name. Enter your current mailing address. Print the name of the city, state or province, and country in which the test center is located, and the center number.

[2] YOUR NAME: <u>Print</u> all the information requested in the boxes at the top of the columns (first four letters of your last name, your first initial, and middle initial), and then fill in completely the appropriate space beneath each entry.

[3] DATE OF BIRTH: Fill in completely the space beside the month in which you were born. Then enter the day of the month on which you were born in the boxes at the top of the columns. Fill in completely the appropriate space beneath each entry. Be sure to treat zeros like any other digit, and to add a zero before any single digit; for example 03, not 3. (Your year of birth is not required on the answer sheet.)

[4] SEX: Fill in completely the appropriate space.

[5] REGISTRATION NUMBER: Copy your registration number from your admission ticket into the boxes at the top of the columns and then fill in completely the appropriate space beneath each entry. Check your admission ticket again to make certain that you have copied your registration number accurately.

[6] TITLE CODE: Copy the numbers shown below and fill in completely the appropriate spaces beneath each entry as shown. When you have completed item 6, check to be sure it is identical to the illustration below.

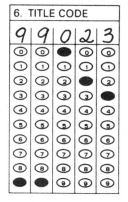

[7] CERTIFICATION STATEMENT: In the boxed area, please write (do not print) the following statement: I certify that I am the person whose name appears on this answer sheet. I also agree not to disclose the contents of the test I am taking today to anyone. Sign and date where indicated.

[8] FORM CODE: Copy *GR 87-6* in the box.

[9] TEST BOOK SERIAL NUMBER: Copy the serial number of your test book in the box. It is printed in red at the upper right on the front cover of your test book.

C. WHEN YOU HAVE FINISHED THESE INSTRUCTIONS, PLEASE TURN YOUR ANSWER SHEET OVER AND SIGN YOUR NAME IN THE BOX EXACTLY AS YOU DID FOR ITEM [7].

When you have finished, wait for further instructions from the supervisor. DO NOT OPEN YOUR TEST BOOK UNTIL YOU ARE TOLD TO DO SO.

FOR GENERAL TEST, FORM GR87-6 ONLY
Answer Key and Percentages* of Examinees Answering Each Question Correctly

VERBAL ABILITY						QUANTITATIVE ABILITY						ANALYTICAL ABILITY					
Section 1			Section 2			Section 3			Section 4			Section 5			Section 6		
Number	Answer	P+	Number	Answer	P+	Number	Answer	P+	Number	Answer	P+	Number	Answer	P+	Number	Answer	P+
1	B	82	1	A	89	1	A	96	1	A	91	1	B	91	1	E	91
2	D	59	2	D	75	2	C	91	2	B	94	2	E	83	2	E	38
3	B	54	3	A	67	3	A	86	3	A	90	3	A	94	3	B	75
4	E	56	4	C	60	4	B	86	4	B	86	4	C	86	4	D	93
5	E	52	5	D	69	5	C	86	5	D	87	5	B	81	5	A	79
6	B	32	6	D	50	6	D	78	6	C	84	6	E	66	6	B	59
7	C	29	7	B	52	7	B	83	7	D	83	7	E	64	7	C	57
8	E	90	8	C	83	8	A	82	8	C	67	8	D	85	8	D	93
9	D	84	9	E	89	9	B	71	9	B	70	9	C	77	9	E	75
10	A	40	10	C	48	10	A	68	10	A	64	10	A	73	10	B	47
11	E	80	11	D	72	11	B	55	11	C	65	11	D	87	11	E	67
12	D	53	12	A	50	12	C	49	12	D	38	12	A	45	12	D	70
13	A	47	13	D	31	13	D	41	13	A	60	13	A	67	13	A	42
14	D	35	14	D	54	14	D	25	14	A	43	14	B	54	14	B	65
15	C	27	15	B	31	15	A	42	15	D	17	15	D	52	15	C	55
16	A	16	16	E	24	16	C	95	16	D	86	16	D	41	16	E	71
17	B	55	17	E	83	17	A	93	17	A	85	17	E	37	17	D	28
18	D	35	18	B	57	18	B	76	18	B	73	18	C	37	18	E	33
19	A	63	19	E	81	19	E	70	19	C	77	19	E	32	19	D	37
20	C	67	20	C	59	20	D	71	20	B	73	20	A	26	20	E	13
21	B	54	21	E	72	21	D	70	21	C	85	21	C	50	21	C	36
22	A	58	22	D	40	22	E	61	22	E	71	22	B	46	22	B	36
23	E	59	23	B	66	23	E	47	23	D	71	23	E	37	23	C	50
24	C	62	24	C	50	24	C	36	24	C	55	24	B	49	24	A	44
25	A	55	25	E	62	25	D	34	25	C	35	25	A	31	25	A	50
26	B	65	26	A	70	26	A	60	26	B	28						
27	E	33	27	E	16	27	B	40	27	E	61						
28	B	91	28	D	94	28	E	60	28	E	43						
29	C	84	29	A	87	29	B	45	29	A	31						
30	A	84	30	B	83	30	C	27	30	A	41						
31	C	72	31	C	51												
32	B	49	32	B	53												
33	A	51	33	C	45												
34	B	31	34	E	45												
35	D	40	35	C	42												
36	D	29	36	D	34												
37	E	24	37	B	32												
38	D	23	38	E	10												

*Estimated P+ for the group of examinees who took the GRE General Test in a recent three-year period.

SCORE CONVERSIONS AND PERCENTS BELOW* for GRE GENERAL TEST, FORM GR87-6 ONLY

Raw Score	Verbal Score	% Below	Quantitative Score	% Below	Analytical Score	% Below	Raw Score	Verbal Score	% Below	Quantitative Score	% Below	Analytical Score	% Below
72-76	800	99					35	410	31	500	37	610	74
71	790	99					34	400	28	490	34	590	69
							33	390	26	480	32	580	67
70	780	99					32	380	24	460	27	560	61
69	760	99					31	370	22	450	26	550	59
68	750	98											
67	740	98					30	360	18	440	23	530	53
66	720	96					29	360	18	430	21	520	50
							28	350	17	410	18	500	44
65	710	96					27	340	15	400	16	490	41
64	700	95					26	330	13	390	14	470	36
63	690	94											
62	680	93					25	330	13	380	13	460	33
61	660	91					24	320	11	360	10	440	27
							23	310	10	350	9	430	25
60	650	89	800	98			22	300	8	340	8	410	21
59	640	88	800	98			21	290	7	330	7	400	18
58	630	86	790	98									
57	620	85	780	97			20	280	6	310	5	380	15
56	610	84	770	95			19	270	4	300	4	370	13
							18	260	3	290	3	350	10
55	600	82	750	92			17	250	3	280	3	340	9
54	590	80	740	90			16	240	2	260	2	320	6
53	580	78	730	89									
52	570	75	720	87			15	230	1	250	1	310	5
51	560	73	700	83			14	220	1	240	1	300	4
							13	210	1	230	1	280	3
50	550	71	690	81	800	99	12	200	0	210	0	270	2
49	540	68	680	79	800	99	11	200	0	200	0	250	1
48	530	65	670	77	800	99							
47	520	63	650	72	790	98	10	200	0	200	0	240	1
46	510	60	640	71	770	98	9	200	0	200	0	220	1
							8	200	0	200	0	210	0
45	500	57	630	68	760	97	0-7	200	0	200	0	200	0
44	490	55	620	65	740	95							
43	480	52	600	61	730	94							
42	470	49	590	59	710	92							
41	460	45	580	56	700	91							
40	450	43	560	52	680	88							
39	440	40	550	49	670	86							
38	430	37	540	46	650	84							
37	420	34	530	44	640	81							
36	420	34	510	39	620	77							

*Percent scoring below the scaled score, based on the performance of the 816,621 examinees who took the General Test between October 1, 1983, and September 30, 1986.

General Test Average Scores for Seniors and Nonenrolled College Graduates, Classified by Intended Graduate Major Field Group
(Based on the performance of GRE examinees who took the General Test between October 1, 1983, and September 30, 1986)

Intended Graduate Major Field Group	Number of Examinees	Verbal Ability	Quantitative Ability	Analytical Ability
HUMANITIES				
Arts	8,696	495	496	532
Languages and Other Humanities	29,808	540	531	553
SOCIAL SCIENCES				
Education	24,042	450	479	506
Behavioral Sciences	58,352	509	525	542
Other Social Sciences	28,401	475	485	512
BIOLOGICAL SCIENCES				
Bioscience	18,838	507	581	569
Health Sciences	32,043	469	504	521
Other Applied Bioscience	10,698	486	553	551
PHYSICAL SCIENCES				
Engineering	33,335	478	674	580
Mathematical Sciences	20,729	490	657	596
Physical Sciences	18,599	518	635	587

GRADUATE RECORD EXAMINATIONS
GENERAL TEST

SIDE 1

Use only a pencil with a soft, black lead (No. 2 or HB) to complete this answer sheet. Be sure to darken completely the space that corresponds to your answer choice. Completely erase any errors or stray marks.

1.
YOUR NAME: (PRINT)
Last Name (Family or Surname)   First Name (Given)   M.I.

MAILING ADDRESS: (PRINT)
Street Address or P.O. Box

City   State or Province   Country   Zip or Postal Code

CENTER: (PRINT)
City   State or Province   Country   Center Number

2. YOUR NAME
First 4 letters of last name | First Init. | Mid. Init.

3. DATE OF BIRTH

Month: Jan., Feb., Mar., Apr., May, June, July, Aug., Sept., Oct., Nov., Dec.

Day

4. SEX ○ Male ○ Female

FOR ETS USE ONLY

5. REGISTRATION NUMBER

6. TITLE CODE

7. CERTIFICATION STATEMENT

SIGNATURE: _____ DATE: _____

8. FORM CODE:

9. TEST BOOK SERIAL NUMBER

BE SURE EACH MARK IS DARK AND COMPLETELY FILLS THE INTENDED SPACE AS ILLUSTRATED HERE: ●.
YOU MAY FIND MORE ANSWER RESPONSES THAN YOU NEED. IF SO, PLEASE LEAVE THEM BLANK.

SECTION 1

Questions 1–42, answer choices A B C D E

SECTION 2

Questions 1–42, answer choices A B C D E

540TF44P420   Q1276 - 04   *Section 3 begins on reverse side.*

GRADUATE RECORD EXAMINATIONS – GENERAL TEST

SIDE 2

SIGNATURE:

Use only a pencil with a soft, black lead (No. 2 or HB) to complete this answer sheet. Be sure to darken completely the space that corresponds to your answer choice. Completely erase any errors or stray marks.

TURN ANSWER SHEET OVER AND BEGIN TEST ON SIDE 1.

YOU MAY FIND MORE ANSWER RESPONSES THAN YOU NEED. IF SO, PLEASE LEAVE THEM BLANK.

SECTION 3	SECTION 4	SECTION 5	SECTION 6	SECTION 7
1 A B C D E	1 A B C D E	1 A B C D E	1 A B C D E	1 A B C D E
2 A B C D E	2 A B C D E	2 A B C D E	2 A B C D E	2 A B C D E
3 A B C D E	3 A B C D E	3 A B C D E	3 A B C D E	3 A B C D E
4 A B C D E	4 A B C D E	4 A B C D E	4 A B C D E	4 A B C D E
5 A B C D E	5 A B C D E	5 A B C D E	5 A B C D E	5 A B C D E
6 A B C D E	6 A B C D E	6 A B C D E	6 A B C D E	6 A B C D E
7 A B C D E	7 A B C D E	7 A B C D E	7 A B C D E	7 A B C D E
8 A B C D E	8 A B C D E	8 A B C D E	8 A B C D E	8 A B C D E
9 A B C D E	9 A B C D E	9 A B C D E	9 A B C D E	9 A B C D E
10 A B C D E	10 A B C D E	10 A B C D E	10 A B C D E	10 A B C D E
11 A B C D E	11 A B C D E	11 A B C D E	11 A B C D E	11 A B C D E
12 A B C D E	12 A B C D E	12 A B C D E	12 A B C D E	12 A B C D E
13 A B C D E	13 A B C D E	13 A B C D E	13 A B C D E	13 A B C D E
14 A B C D E	14 A B C D E	14 A B C D E	14 A B C D E	14 A B C D E
15 A B C D E	15 A B C D E	15 A B C D E	15 A B C D E	15 A B C D E
16 A B C D E	16 A B C D E	16 A B C D E	16 A B C D E	16 A B C D E
17 A B C D E	17 A B C D E	17 A B C D E	17 A B C D E	17 A B C D E
18 A B C D E	18 A B C D E	18 A B C D E	18 A B C D E	18 A B C D E
19 A B C D E	19 A B C D E	19 A B C D E	19 A B C D E	19 A B C D E
20 A B C D E	20 A B C D E	20 A B C D E	20 A B C D E	20 A B C D E
21 A B C D E	21 A B C D E	21 A B C D E	21 A B C D E	21 A B C D E
22 A B C D E	22 A B C D E	22 A B C D E	22 A B C D E	22 A B C D E
23 A B C D E	23 A B C D E	23 A B C D E	23 A B C D E	23 A B C D E
24 A B C D E	24 A B C D E	24 A B C D E	24 A B C D E	24 A B C D E
25 A B C D E	25 A B C D E	25 A B C D E	25 A B C D E	25 A B C D E
26 A B C D E	26 A B C D E	26 A B C D E	26 A B C D E	26 A B C D E
27 A B C D E	27 A B C D E	27 A B C D E	27 A B C D E	27 A B C D E
28 A B C D E	28 A B C D E	28 A B C D E	28 A B C D E	28 A B C D E
29 A B C D E	29 A B C D E	29 A B C D E	29 A B C D E	29 A B C D E
30 A B C D E	30 A B C D E	30 A B C D E	30 A B C D E	30 A B C D E
31 A B C D E	31 A B C D E	31 A B C D E	31 A B C D E	31 A B C D E
32 A B C D E	32 A B C D E	32 A B C D E	32 A B C D E	32 A B C D E
33 A B C D E	33 A B C D E	33 A B C D E	33 A B C D E	33 A B C D E
34 A B C D E	34 A B C D E	34 A B C D E	34 A B C D E	34 A B C D E
35 A B C D E	35 A B C D E	35 A B C D E	35 A B C D E	35 A B C D E
36 A B C D E	36 A B C D E	36 A B C D E	36 A B C D E	36 A B C D E
37 A B C D E	37 A B C D E	37 A B C D E	37 A B C D E	37 A B C D E
38 A B C D E	38 A B C D E	38 A B C D E	38 A B C D E	38 A B C D E
39 A B C D E	39 A B C D E	39 A B C D E	39 A B C D E	39 A B C D E
40 A B C D E	40 A B C D E	40 A B C D E	40 A B C D E	40 A B C D E
41 A B C D E	41 A B C D E	41 A B C D E	41 A B C D E	41 A B C D E
42 A B C D E	42 A B C D E	42 A B C D E	42 A B C D E	42 A B C D E

GRADUATE RECORD EXAMINATIONS
GENERAL TEST

SIDE 1

Use only a pencil with a soft, black lead (No. 2 or HB) to complete this answer sheet. Be sure to darken completely the space that corresponds to your answer choice. Completely erase any errors or stray marks.

1.
YOUR NAME: _____
(PRINT)   Last Name (Family or Surname)   First Name (Given)   M.I.

MAILING ADDRESS: _____
(PRINT)

_____
City   State or Province   Country   Zip or Postal Code

CENTER: _____
(PRINT)   City   State or Province   Country   Center Number

2. YOUR NAME

First 4 letters of last name | First Init. | Mid. Init.

3. DATE OF BIRTH

Month | Day

Jan.
Feb.
Mar.
Apr.
May
June
July
Aug.
Sept.
Oct.
Nov.
Dec.

4. SEX ◯ Male ◯ Female

FOR ETS USE ONLY

5. REGISTRATION NUMBER

6. TITLE CODE

7. CERTIFICATION STATEMENT

_____

_____

_____

_____

_____

_____

SIGNATURE: _____   DATE: _____

8. FORM CODE: _____

9. TEST BOOK SERIAL NUMBER

_____

BE SURE EACH MARK IS DARK AND COMPLETELY FILLS THE INTENDED SPACE AS ILLUSTRATED HERE: ● .
YOU MAY FIND MORE ANSWER RESPONSES THAN YOU NEED. IF SO, PLEASE LEAVE THEM BLANK.

SECTION 1

(Answer grid numbered 1 through 42, choices A B C D E)

SECTION 2

(Answer grid numbered 1 through 42, choices A B C D E)

540TF44P420   Q1276 · 04

Section 3 begins on reverse side.

GRADUATE RECORD EXAMINATIONS – GENERAL TEST

SIDE 2

SIGNATURE: ______________________________

Use only a pencil with a soft, black lead (No. 2 or HB) to complete this answer sheet. Be sure to darken completely the space that corresponds to your answer choice. Completely erase any errors or stray marks.

TURN ANSWER SHEET OVER AND BEGIN TEST ON SIDE 1.

YOU MAY FIND MORE ANSWER RESPONSES THAN YOU NEED. IF SO, PLEASE LEAVE THEM BLANK.

	SECTION 3	SECTION 4	SECTION 5	SECTION 6	SECTION 7
1	A B C D E	A B C D E	A B C D E	A B C D E	A B C D E
2	A B C D E	A B C D E	A B C D E	A B C D E	A B C D E
3	A B C D E	A B C D E	A B C D E	A B C D E	A B C D E
4	A B C D E	A B C D E	A B C D E	A B C D E	A B C D E
5	A B C D E	A B C D E	A B C D E	A B C D E	A B C D E
6	A B C D E	A B C D E	A B C D E	A B C D E	A B C D E
7	A B C D E	A B C D E	A B C D E	A B C D E	A B C D E
8	A B C D E	A B C D E	A B C D E	A B C D E	A B C D E
9	A B C D E	A B C D E	A B C D E	A B C D E	A B C D E
10	A B C D E	A B C D E	A B C D E	A B C D E	A B C D E
11	A B C D E	A B C D E	A B C D E	A B C D E	A B C D E
12	A B C D E	A B C D E	A B C D E	A B C D E	A B C D E
13	A B C D E	A B C D E	A B C D E	A B C D E	A B C D E
14	A B C D E	A B C D E	A B C D E	A B C D E	A B C D E
15	A B C D E	A B C D E	A B C D E	A B C D E	A B C D E
16	A B C D E	A B C D E	A B C D E	A B C D E	A B C D E
17	A B C D E	A B C D E	A B C D E	A B C D E	A B C D E
18	A B C D E	A B C D E	A B C D E	A B C D E	A B C D E
19	A B C D E	A B C D E	A B C D E	A B C D E	A B C D E
20	A B C D E	A B C D E	A B C D E	A B C D E	A B C D E
21	A B C D E	A B C D E	A B C D E	A B C D E	A B C D E
22	A B C D E	A B C D E	A B C D E	A B C D E	A B C D E
23	A B C D E	A B C D E	A B C D E	A B C D E	A B C D E
24	A B C D E	A B C D E	A B C D E	A B C D E	A B C D E
25	A B C D E	A B C D E	A B C D E	A B C D E	A B C D E
26	A B C D E	A B C D E	A B C D E	A B C D E	A B C D E
27	A B C D E	A B C D E	A B C D E	A B C D E	A B C D E
28	A B C D E	A B C D E	A B C D E	A B C D E	A B C D E
29	A B C D E	A B C D E	A B C D E	A B C D E	A B C D E
30	A B C D E	A B C D E	A B C D E	A B C D E	A B C D E
31	A B C D E	A B C D E	A B C D E	A B C D E	A B C D E
32	A B C D E	A B C D E	A B C D E	A B C D E	A B C D E
33	A B C D E	A B C D E	A B C D E	A B C D E	A B C D E
34	A B C D E	A B C D E	A B C D E	A B C D E	A B C D E
35	A B C D E	A B C D E	A B C D E	A B C D E	A B C D E
36	A B C D E	A B C D E	A B C D E	A B C D E	A B C D E
37	A B C D E	A B C D E	A B C D E	A B C D E	A B C D E
38	A B C D E	A B C D E	A B C D E	A B C D E	A B C D E
39	A B C D E	A B C D E	A B C D E	A B C D E	A B C D E
40	A B C D E	A B C D E	A B C D E	A B C D E	A B C D E
41	A B C D E	A B C D E	A B C D E	A B C D E	A B C D E
42	A B C D E	A B C D E	A B C D E	A B C D E	A B C D E

GRADUATE RECORD EXAMINATIONS
GENERAL TEST

SIDE 1

Use only a pencil with a soft, black lead (No. 2 or HB) to complete this answer sheet. Be sure to darken completely the space that corresponds to your answer choice. Completely erase any errors or stray marks.

1. YOUR NAME: (PRINT)
Last Name (Family or Surname)   First Name (Given)   M.I.

MAILING ADDRESS: (PRINT)
Street Address or P.O. Box

City   State or Province   Country   Zip or Postal Code

CENTER: (PRINT)
City   State or Province   Country   Center Number

2. YOUR NAME
First 4 letters of last name | First Init. | Mid. Init.

3. DATE OF BIRTH

Month	Day
Jan.	
Feb.	
Mar.	
Apr.	
May	
June	
July	
Aug.	
Sept.	
Oct.	
Nov.	
Dec.	

4. SEX ○ Male ○ Female

FOR ETS USE ONLY

5. REGISTRATION NUMBER

6. TITLE CODE

7. CERTIFICATION STATEMENT

SIGNATURE: _____ DATE: _____

8. FORM CODE:

9. TEST BOOK SERIAL NUMBER

BE SURE EACH MARK IS DARK AND COMPLETELY FILLS THE INTENDED SPACE AS ILLUSTRATED HERE: ●.
YOU MAY FIND MORE ANSWER RESPONSES THAN YOU NEED. IF SO, PLEASE LEAVE THEM BLANK.

SECTION 1

(Answer bubbles 1–42, options A B C D E)

SECTION 2

(Answer bubbles 1–42, options A B C D E)

GRADUATE RECORD EXAMINATIONS – GENERAL TEST

SIDE 2

SIGNATURE: ______________________________

Use only a pencil with a soft, black lead (No. 2 or HB) to complete this answer sheet. Be sure to darken completely the space that corresponds to your answer choice. Completely erase any errors or stray marks.

TURN ANSWER SHEET OVER AND BEGIN TEST ON SIDE 1.

YOU MAY FIND MORE ANSWER RESPONSES THAN YOU NEED. IF SO, PLEASE LEAVE THEM BLANK.

SECTION 3	SECTION 4	SECTION 5	SECTION 6	SECTION 7
1 (A) (B) (C) (D) (E)	1 (A) (B) (C) (D) (E)	1 (A) (B) (C) (D) (E)	1 (A) (B) (C) (D) (E)	1 (A) (B) (C) (D) (E)
2 (A) (B) (C) (D) (E)	2 (A) (B) (C) (D) (E)	2 (A) (B) (C) (D) (E)	2 (A) (B) (C) (D) (E)	2 (A) (B) (C) (D) (E)
3 (A) (B) (C) (D) (E)	3 (A) (B) (C) (D) (E)	3 (A) (B) (C) (D) (E)	3 (A) (B) (C) (D) (E)	3 (A) (B) (C) (D) (E)
4 (A) (B) (C) (D) (E)	4 (A) (B) (C) (D) (E)	4 (A) (B) (C) (D) (E)	4 (A) (B) (C) (D) (E)	4 (A) (B) (C) (D) (E)
5 (A) (B) (C) (D) (E)	5 (A) (B) (C) (D) (E)	5 (A) (B) (C) (D) (E)	5 (A) (B) (C) (D) (E)	5 (A) (B) (C) (D) (E)
6 (A) (B) (C) (D) (E)	6 (A) (B) (C) (D) (E)	6 (A) (B) (C) (D) (E)	6 (A) (B) (C) (D) (E)	6 (A) (B) (C) (D) (E)
7 (A) (B) (C) (D) (E)	7 (A) (B) (C) (D) (E)	7 (A) (B) (C) (D) (E)	7 (A) (B) (C) (D) (E)	7 (A) (B) (C) (D) (E)
8 (A) (B) (C) (D) (E)	8 (A) (B) (C) (D) (E)	8 (A) (B) (C) (D) (E)	8 (A) (B) (C) (D) (E)	8 (A) (B) (C) (D) (E)
9 (A) (B) (C) (D) (E)	9 (A) (B) (C) (D) (E)	9 (A) (B) (C) (D) (E)	9 (A) (B) (C) (D) (E)	9 (A) (B) (C) (D) (E)
10 (A) (B) (C) (D) (E)	10 (A) (B) (C) (D) (E)	10 (A) (B) (C) (D) (E)	10 (A) (B) (C) (D) (E)	10 (A) (B) (C) (D) (E)
11 (A) (B) (C) (D) (E)	11 (A) (B) (C) (D) (E)	11 (A) (B) (C) (D) (E)	11 (A) (B) (C) (D) (E)	11 (A) (B) (C) (D) (E)
12 (A) (B) (C) (D) (E)	12 (A) (B) (C) (D) (E)	12 (A) (B) (C) (D) (E)	12 (A) (B) (C) (D) (E)	12 (A) (B) (C) (D) (E)
13 (A) (B) (C) (D) (E)	13 (A) (B) (C) (D) (E)	13 (A) (B) (C) (D) (E)	13 (A) (B) (C) (D) (E)	13 (A) (B) (C) (D) (E)
14 (A) (B) (C) (D) (E)	14 (A) (B) (C) (D) (E)	14 (A) (B) (C) (D) (E)	14 (A) (B) (C) (D) (E)	14 (A) (B) (C) (D) (E)
15 (A) (B) (C) (D) (E)	15 (A) (B) (C) (D) (E)	15 (A) (B) (C) (D) (E)	15 (A) (B) (C) (D) (E)	15 (A) (B) (C) (D) (E)
16 (A) (B) (C) (D) (E)	16 (A) (B) (C) (D) (E)	16 (A) (B) (C) (D) (E)	16 (A) (B) (C) (D) (E)	16 (A) (B) (C) (D) (E)
17 (A) (B) (C) (D) (E)	17 (A) (B) (C) (D) (E)	17 (A) (B) (C) (D) (E)	17 (A) (B) (C) (D) (E)	17 (A) (B) (C) (D) (E)
18 (A) (B) (C) (D) (E)	18 (A) (B) (C) (D) (E)	18 (A) (B) (C) (D) (E)	18 (A) (B) (C) (D) (E)	18 (A) (B) (C) (D) (E)
19 (A) (B) (C) (D) (E)	19 (A) (B) (C) (D) (E)	19 (A) (B) (C) (D) (E)	19 (A) (B) (C) (D) (E)	19 (A) (B) (C) (D) (E)
20 (A) (B) (C) (D) (E)	20 (A) (B) (C) (D) (E)	20 (A) (B) (C) (D) (E)	20 (A) (B) (C) (D) (E)	20 (A) (B) (C) (D) (E)
21 (A) (B) (C) (D) (E)	21 (A) (B) (C) (D) (E)	21 (A) (B) (C) (D) (E)	21 (A) (B) (C) (D) (E)	21 (A) (B) (C) (D) (E)
22 (A) (B) (C) (D) (E)	22 (A) (B) (C) (D) (E)	22 (A) (B) (C) (D) (E)	22 (A) (B) (C) (D) (E)	22 (A) (B) (C) (D) (E)
23 (A) (B) (C) (D) (E)	23 (A) (B) (C) (D) (E)	23 (A) (B) (C) (D) (E)	23 (A) (B) (C) (D) (E)	23 (A) (B) (C) (D) (E)
24 (A) (B) (C) (D) (E)	24 (A) (B) (C) (D) (E)	24 (A) (B) (C) (D) (E)	24 (A) (B) (C) (D) (E)	24 (A) (B) (C) (D) (E)
25 (A) (B) (C) (D) (E)	25 (A) (B) (C) (D) (E)	25 (A) (B) (C) (D) (E)	25 (A) (B) (C) (D) (E)	25 (A) (B) (C) (D) (E)
26 (A) (B) (C) (D) (E)	26 (A) (B) (C) (D) (E)	26 (A) (B) (C) (D) (E)	26 (A) (B) (C) (D) (E)	26 (A) (B) (C) (D) (E)
27 (A) (B) (C) (D) (E)	27 (A) (B) (C) (D) (E)	27 (A) (B) (C) (D) (E)	27 (A) (B) (C) (D) (E)	27 (A) (B) (C) (D) (E)
28 (A) (B) (C) (D) (E)	28 (A) (B) (C) (D) (E)	28 (A) (B) (C) (D) (E)	28 (A) (B) (C) (D) (E)	28 (A) (B) (C) (D) (E)
29 (A) (B) (C) (D) (E)	29 (A) (B) (C) (D) (E)	29 (A) (B) (C) (D) (E)	29 (A) (B) (C) (D) (E)	29 (A) (B) (C) (D) (E)
30 (A) (B) (C) (D) (E)	30 (A) (B) (C) (D) (E)	30 (A) (B) (C) (D) (E)	30 (A) (B) (C) (D) (E)	30 (A) (B) (C) (D) (E)
31 (A) (B) (C) (D) (E)	31 (A) (B) (C) (D) (E)	31 (A) (B) (C) (D) (E)	31 (A) (B) (C) (D) (E)	31 (A) (B) (C) (D) (E)
32 (A) (B) (C) (D) (E)	32 (A) (B) (C) (D) (E)	32 (A) (B) (C) (D) (E)	32 (A) (B) (C) (D) (E)	32 (A) (B) (C) (D) (E)
33 (A) (B) (C) (D) (E)	33 (A) (B) (C) (D) (E)	33 (A) (B) (C) (D) (E)	33 (A) (B) (C) (D) (E)	33 (A) (B) (C) (D) (E)
34 (A) (B) (C) (D) (E)	34 (A) (B) (C) (D) (E)	34 (A) (B) (C) (D) (E)	34 (A) (B) (C) (D) (E)	34 (A) (B) (C) (D) (E)
35 (A) (B) (C) (D) (E)	35 (A) (B) (C) (D) (E)	35 (A) (B) (C) (D) (E)	35 (A) (B) (C) (D) (E)	35 (A) (B) (C) (D) (E)
36 (A) (B) (C) (D) (E)	36 (A) (B) (C) (D) (E)	36 (A) (B) (C) (D) (E)	36 (A) (B) (C) (D) (E)	36 (A) (B) (C) (D) (E)
37 (A) (B) (C) (D) (E)	37 (A) (B) (C) (D) (E)	37 (A) (B) (C) (D) (E)	37 (A) (B) (C) (D) (E)	37 (A) (B) (C) (D) (E)
38 (A) (B) (C) (D) (E)	38 (A) (B) (C) (D) (E)	38 (A) (B) (C) (D) (E)	38 (A) (B) (C) (D) (E)	38 (A) (B) (C) (D) (E)
39 (A) (B) (C) (D) (E)	39 (A) (B) (C) (D) (E)	39 (A) (B) (C) (D) (E)	39 (A) (B) (C) (D) (E)	39 (A) (B) (C) (D) (E)
40 (A) (B) (C) (D) (E)	40 (A) (B) (C) (D) (E)	40 (A) (B) (C) (D) (E)	40 (A) (B) (C) (D) (E)	40 (A) (B) (C) (D) (E)
41 (A) (B) (C) (D) (E)	41 (A) (B) (C) (D) (E)	41 (A) (B) (C) (D) (E)	41 (A) (B) (C) (D) (E)	41 (A) (B) (C) (D) (E)
42 (A) (B) (C) (D) (E)	42 (A) (B) (C) (D) (E)	42 (A) (B) (C) (D) (E)	42 (A) (B) (C) (D) (E)	42 (A) (B) (C) (D) (E)

GRE® PUBLICATIONS ORDER FORM

Graduate Record Examinations
Educational Testing Service
CN 6014
Princeton, NJ 08541-6014

Please check the appropriate box(es).

☐ Personal order; payment enclosed.
☐ Institution order
    ☐ Payment enclosed
    ☐ Purchase order enclosed

Remittance should be made payable to Graduate Record Examinations.

DATE OF THIS ORDER

Item Number	Publication	Price	No. of Copies	Amount	Postage*	Total
	Software Editions (540-07)					
299625	Practicing to Take the GRE General Test—No. 4, Apple Macintosh Software Edition	$55.00				
299626	Practicing to Take the GRE General Test—No. 4, IBM Software Edition	55.00				
	Practice Test Books (540-01)					
241230	†Practicing to Take the GRE General Test—No. 5	7.00				
241216	Practicing to Take the GRE General Test—No. 4	7.00				
241223	Practicing to Take the GRE Biology Test	6.00				
241224	Practicing to Take the GRE Chemistry Test	6.00				
241217	Practicing to Take the GRE Computer Science Test	6.00				
241218	Practicing to Take the GRE Economics Test	6.00				
241211	Practicing to Take the GRE Education Test	6.00				
241221	Practicing to Take the GRE Engineering Test	6.00				
241227	†Practicing to Take the GRE Geology Test	6.00				
241219	Practicing to Take the GRE History Test	6.00				
241225	Practicing to Take the GRE Literature in English Test	6.00				
241228	†Practicing to Take the GRE Mathematics Test	6.00				
241220	Practicing to Take the GRE Physics Test	6.00				
241222	Practicing to Take the GRE Psychology Test	6.00				
241229	†Practicing to Take the GRE Sociology Test	6.00				
	Directory of Graduate Programs (540-98)					
252020	†Volume A—Agriculture, Biological Sciences, Psychology, Health Sciences, and Home Economics	10.00				
252021	†Volume B—Arts and Humanities	10.00				
252022	†Volume C—Physical Sciences, Mathematics, and Engineering	10.00				
252023	†Volume D—Social Sciences and Education	10.00				

*Postage and handling to a single address in North America, U.S. Possessions, or APO addresses is $3 for the first book ordered and $1 for each additional book. Add $5 for each software edition ordered.

To all other locations (airmail only) to a single address, add $7 for the first book ordered and $5 for each additional book. Add $15 for each software edition ordered.

†Available September 1987.

Payment should be made by check or money order drawn on a U.S. bank, U.S. Postal Money Order, UNESCO Coupons, or International Postal Reply Coupons.

Orders received without payment or purchase order will be returned.

⬆ **Total** ⬆
Amount Due

TYPE OR PRINT CLEARLY BELOW. DO NOT DETACH THESE MAILING LABELS.

Graduate Record Examinations
Educational Testing Service
CN 6014
Princeton, NJ 08541-6014

TO: _____

_____

_____

_____

Graduate Record Examinations
Educational Testing Service
CN 6014
Princeton, NJ 08541-6014

TO: _____

_____

_____

_____